When the Princess Dies...

When the Princess Dies...

A Fairy Tale for Women
With Practical Tools for Transforming and Healing the Father-Daughter Relationship

Bobbie Berg, PhD

Mill City Press

Minneapolis, MN

Copyright © 2015 by Bobbie Berg

Mill City Press, Inc.
322 First Avenue N, 5th floor
Minneapolis, MN 55401
612.455.2293
www.millcitypublishing.com

ISBN-13: 978-1-63413-246-6
LCCN: 2014922777

Cover Design by Alan Pranke
Typeset by Sophie Chi

Printed in the United States of America

in the capability to be more kind towards herself and others. I highly recommend this book for all women who want to break the bitter cycle of the father-daughter wound and celebrate their womanhood."

—Linda Metzger, M.A., Marriage and Family Therapist

"An enlightening and eye-opening read! As a father, I was surprised by how much I enjoyed this book. I found Berg's style to be extremely down-to-earth and non-judgmental—almost warming in its tone. But best of all was the way the author interspersed psychological explanation with a marvelous metaphorical fairy tale. The approach was not only unique, but also incredibly effective in getting points across in an interesting and empowering manner. This allows a woman to channel her own childhood in a way that is a most constructive stepping stone on her path to healing. At the same time, fathers can come to understand the impact of the role they play in their daughters' lives. An important book."

—John D. Harris, educator

"Dr. Berg brings a unique format to a difficult, painful topic in which she entertains the reader while simultaneously providing significant guidelines, which can heal troubled daughter/father interactions. She successfully draws a parallel between an adult fairy tale and the reality of certain malfunctioning relationships. It's a must-read for women who wish and need to take charge of their own emotional well-being."

—Claudette Young, author; member,
Ventura County Writers Club

"I believe this book captures the emotions of all those suffering from father-loss. Every sentence feels like Dr. Berg is speaking to me personally. I now realize that I need all of my parts to go on my journey to integration: The Wise Woman, The Maiden, The Inner Child, The Man, and even The Judge."

—Lilly Smith, Princess Frog

"As I read this book, I began to realize, and maybe for the first time, how the relationship with my father has affected my life. Most often a woman recognizes the influence and the ties she has had or not had with her mother, but the parallel this book draws with The Princess Frog and reality is a real awakening. The writing is clear; the concepts and exercises in the back are easy to understand. I highly recommend *When the Princess Dies* for women who are struggling with father issues."

—Jody Avery-Smith, published author; Princess Frog

"To say that it was a privilege to read Dr. Berg's book is an understatement. It is, indeed … brilliant. It demonstrates her wealth of experience in the field of psychology and as such, distills trust in the reader. *When the Princess Dies* is an important self-help book for women of all ages who have had or continue to have complex father-wounding issues and need to move on with more productive and healthier lives. The author's narrative is unique, colorfully imaginative, and understandable. I predict this original slant on an old theme can and will turn lives around. I highly recommend it."

—Kathleen Auth, artist; author

"This is years of therapy in one book. Thank you, Dr. Berg, for compiling this comprehensive guide to wellness. It will be of benefit to so many women with a history of father-daughter issues."

—M. R., M. S., psychotherapist; Princess Frog

"As a dad who has raised four loving daughters, I especially applaud Dr. Berg's insights in *The Good Father* section of the book. While some fathers may intuit the guidelines presented, others will gain valuable insight into the important aspects of their role and behavior with respect to their daughters. The payback can be unbelievably moving when you see them grow into strong, independent, yet obviously feminine women. It was so gratifying when one of my daughters, now wife and mother, recently thanked me for the respect, encouragement, and guidance I gave her as she was growing up, which she said had an incredibly positive impact on her life. This book does a great service by documenting the basic role and behavior guidelines for fathers raising daughters."

—Norm Ohren, father of daughters

"*When the Princess Dies* is an engaging and enlightening fairy tale, which addresses a woman's healing from an unhealthy father-daughter relationship. It is a good read for both mental health professionals and lay people, with cogent explanations woven into the story."

—Rochelle Linick, freelance writer

"What can I say about this magical book? Throughout my life, I have had unusual relationships with men. I create a protective barrier, a distance, in order to guarantee that if things don't go well, I won't be crushed. Dr. Berg's book provided valuable insight into The Princess Frog part of my inner self and how a dysfunctional relationship with my father has affected every aspect of my life. This newfound clarity, delivered in such a creative way, is seeping in; and exciting subtle changes are occurring."

—H.A.Z., retired architectural designer; Princess Frog

"Good job! I like the storytelling aspects of *When the Princess Dies*, which cultivate wonderful images. The book is useful for women with father issues, especially those new to therapy. I highly endorse it."

—Paulette Dwyer, M.A., psychotherapist; Princess Frog

For all The Princess Frogs …
May you find healing and peace.

Contents

Acknowledgments

It is with deep appreciation I wish to acknowledge the following individuals:

First and foremost, creative teacher, gifted psychotherapist, mentor, and colleague, Dr. Lois "Lo" Sprague, for her expertise, her knowledge, and her loving support in the past. She is at the heart of this narrative; there would be no book without her.

The courageous women who shared their thoughts, feelings, and drawings with me that serve to enrich the material.

Members of my writers' group, past and present, for their incalculable guidance and feedback: Kathleen Auth, Jody Avery-Smith, Audrey Bishop, Jean Castaing, Shelley Linick, Rhoda Novak, Alice Rene, and Claudette Young.

Respected psychotherapists and colleagues: Sandra Greenfeld, PhD; Paulette Dwyer, M.A.; Linda Metzger, M.A.; and Marsha Roberts, M.S.; as well as: Hilary Katersky, Susan Drapkin, Lilly Smith, and, in particular, Kathleen Auth … all for agreeing to read the final material before publication. Also Dean Stevens, Norm Ohren and Christopher Gibson for their valuable contributions from the male perspective.

Jonathan Young, PhD, creator of The Center for Story and Symbol, who has entertained and enlightened me with his excellent seminars on the value and gift of fairytales, myths and film. His stories offered me wonderful maps with which to guide my clients, and helped awaken in me the idea of writing my own fairy tale.

My family, including my wonderful sons Dean and Ross ... also writers ... who encouraged and inspired me. But most especially my husband Gene, for having been The Good Father to our daughter, Mari, and for taking on the role of my cheerleader over fifty years ago, never failing to spur me on.

Foreword

By Sandra Greenfeld, PhD

I am honored to write the foreword for this book.

A licensed psychotherapist for thirty-two years, I have had the privilege of working with a variety of individuals, from small children to adults. Many were women who, growing up, had struggled in the relationships with their fathers. These, as well as those I encountered as a university professor in the Child Mental Health Specialist Program at California State University in Northridge, afforded me the opportunity to become acquainted first-hand with the ill effects fathers could have on their daughters, often impacting every aspect of their lives.

As the fields of psychology and psychiatry have matured, and research techniques have improved in more recent years, we are now recognizing the impact made by fathers on the emotional development of their daughters. Studies show that a woman's success in life and how she views herself can often be directly related to her relationship with her father.

I have known Dr. Bobbie Berg for several years, and as colleagues, we have shared many ideas on the therapeutic practices in the fields of psychology and psychotherapy. Dr. Berg is completely devoted to the subject of the father-daughter relationship. In her fine book, *When the Princess Dies*, she has taken her therapeutic skills of close to thirty years and made them available to a new generation of women. Her dedication as a seasoned therapist and her intriguing approach, have garnered her respect from both her patients and her peers.

Unlike most books on the subject, this one presents something unique: a metaphoric narrative in fairy tale form, of those relationships in which men fall short in their role as fathers. The impact on the daughter is presented, and psychological explanations of the text are incorporated. This helps the reader become aware of what is occurring every step of the way. Appendices offer tips, tools, and self-help exercises that enhance the material and create a path for healing.

This book is worth reading. It is sensitively drawn, respectful of its audience, clever, creative, and entertaining in its delivery, as well as practical in its application. I highly recommend it as a lifeline for those women who would like to come out from under the cloud of father-wounding to lead a more productive, satisfying existence. It offers the reader meaningful insights and important suggestions for one's own metamorphosis from a fearful, self-effacing, self-punishing, unsuccessful woman, to a more content, self-fulfilled one.

Speaking as a psychotherapist in the field for over a quarter of a century, I feel strongly that this book has a place in today's world among the many who find getting through the demands of life and being a woman, difficult indeed. I applaud Dr. Berg for helping to bring to light the importance of the father-daughter relationship and offering hope to those who have been hurt by it.

Preface

In writing this book, I drew on my many years of private practice. With experience, I recognized certain patterns of emotions and behaviors associated with father-wounding. As adults, these women often sought therapy for other issues. For example, they may have felt unfulfilled, sad, or powerless. Had a gnawing sense of something amiss. They might have noticed that anger, even rage, lay just below the surface. Perhaps people had told them they were controlling. Suicidal thoughts plagued their waking hours. They had trust issues. Men issues. They had tumultuous relationships, or no meaningful relationships. Whatever the presenting problem, all were mired in pain.

Through trial and error, I learned which interventions were effective and let go of those that were not. Along with psychotherapy, I conducted several interview/drawing sessions to help me understand more fully the nature of the wounding these women experienced. I sensed these individuals were involved in an important journey. A spiritual one. I found that those who were committed to the work of therapy reaped the benefits and moved on to live more gratifying lives.

In an effort to reach out and be of help to women I'll never meet, I wrote this book based on my experiences with those I cared about, who thought enough of themselves to seek help, and who enriched and humbled me as a human being.

Greek Mythology tells the story of the Titan, Cronos, who devours his children, including three daughters, fearing they will take his place as primary god of the universe. In the fairy tale, Cinderella, a father is depicted as weak, leaving his daughter in the hands of a wicked stepmother. The Bible speaks of Jacob, who, when he hears his daughter Dinah has been raped, falls silent and does nothing.

That there should be found countless stories of daughter abuse by fathers in all cultures throughout history, is no accident. Myths, fairy tales, and Biblical stories reflective of real life, reveal fathers who abandon their daughters in a variety of ways.

It is in that spirit I have created a fairy tale. It is the story of a princess who, because of her father's abandoning his "Good Father" role, turns into a lowly frog ... a "Princess Frog" to be exact. She must then find her way to a better place ... one of healing and wholeness. In this narrative, I have woven fable and fact in an unmistakable pairing of the symbolic and the psychological. Metaphor is enhanced through explanation, and vice versa.

Why specifically a fairy tale? Fairy tales are said to be windows into the human psyche. They provide an inner map of our emotional experiences and of the repair and growth that can occur. They address human themes and can teach life lessons. We recognize ourselves and our struggles in fairy tales. If not consciously, then certainly unconsciously.

Following the fairy tale, the book addresses the concept of The Princess Frog: how she develops, some of her characteristics in relation to men, and ideas on how she can heal.

A description of The Good Father offers the reader the opportunity to become acquainted with the role of the healthy, loving father. Appendices in the back support the fairy tale with additional information including tips, exercises, and an art project completed by several Princess Frogs.

Who will benefit from reading my book? *When the Princess Dies* is written for women who have been wounded by their fathers, are unable to move forward, and wish to heal. It is for those daughters who began with a positive experience in their relationship with their fathers, only to lose it at some point. The text can also be helpful to those who, for whatever reason, never had a loving father-daughter relationship. Furthermore, I invite fathers to educate themselves regarding the importance and power of their role as well as the impact their behavior did, does, or will have on their daughters.

Please note that for those severe cases in which daughters endured horrendous abuse at the hands of their fathers, often for years, this book will be limited. Though it may serve to offer some solace and perhaps even open the door to some healing, it will not take the place of professional help.

Just when the caterpillar thought the world was over,
it became a butterfly.

—anonymous

Introduction

Do you need help overcoming the effects of the negative relationship you had with your father when you were growing up?

Do you find yourself unable to fully trust men in particular? Do you test them? Succumb to them? Toy with them? Seduce them? Reject them?

Are you clueless about how your experience with your father may be related to your tendency to overachieve or underachieve, be controlling or controlled, seek excessive closeness or distance, pursue constant attention or isolation?

If you have answered yes to any of these questions, you have some of the characteristics of what I call The Princess Frog ... a woman who has been wounded by her father.

With the help of this book:

- You will learn how to identify the parts of yourself that serve you and those that betray you.
- You will discover ways in which you may better understand and protect yourself in relationships.
- You will have the opportunity to master the five essential techniques to growth and healing:

1. Self-Awareness
2. Trusting your instincts
3. Meeting your challenges
4. Staying on track
5. Honoring your unique self

I wrote this book because you need a way to emerge from the pain of the abandonment by your father of his Good Father role. Within these pages, lies a map to help lead you out of dark despair into the light of recovery.

The book is designed to be viewed in the order in which it is presented. I recommend reading all the way through the fairy tale first (along with the accompanying explanation) before flipping to the appendices. This will help you get a feel for the whole story before exploring additional information and exercises. Here is an example of the fable-explanation format, which you can expect to encounter in the fairy tale. The following is taken from the text:

> **Once inside the woods, the frog felt dwarfed by the endless array of looming trees. She tried to find her way back to the pond in the shadowy light, but couldn't. She thought about moving ahead, or perhaps going left or right. Instead, she sat motionless on the soft, moist soil in that desolate place between forwards, backwards, and sideways.**

Entering the process of healing and recovery, the daughter finds she cannot go back … . She has crossed over a line, and that experience has changed her. She no longer fits the old mode, yet has not progressed to a new one. She is in limbo.

Let's not keep her there for long! Come journey with me to see the way fathers play a significant role in the mental health of their daughters, and how The Princess Frog learns to move forward on the road to growth and healing.

Chapter One

A Woman's Fairy Tale of Transformation and Healing

Long Ago in Days of Yore ...

Here and there and far away –
In days back then like days today,
The Princess, His Highness will betray;
Her death shall be the price to pay.

Lived a King One Could Adore.

The Princess thinks the King is grand –
Magic sovereign of the land!
God-like does he take command
And gently leads her by the hand.

Yet, the Princess He Banished ...

Suddenly (or so it seems),
The King is dashing all her dreams!
Lightning from the castle streams –
Then flickers out with quiet screams.

Alas! She Just ...Vanished!

Long since gone, the Princess Fair
Dissolved away in her despair.
Instead, a frog is crouching there –
Lost behind a wounded stare.

Will She Be a Frog 'Evermore?

For a kiss is what she'll often long
To break the spell and fix the wrong.
But she herself can leap up strong,
And change her croaks into a song.

nce upon a time, in a faraway land where the sun cast its light on curly trees and lacy flowers, where ladybugs played with newborn kittens and babies' toes, lived a young and beautiful princess. Her home was an enchanting castle made of brown sugar, peacock feathers, and warm snow. The graceful butter-colored spires of the castle reached like tiny fingers toward the lavender sky. The pink flags, which stood atop the spires, touched the white wooly clouds and waved to the birds.

The princess felt happy and safe, for she lived in the castle with her father, the king, who adored her. Often they would spend time on the hillsides flying kites, giggling, and playing hide and seek. The king would then tell her stories until she fell asleep in the silky clover.

The journey begins with a young daughter who shares a wonder-filled relationship with her father. They are close and she feels special ... like a princess. She sees her father as a god or king who will be there to love and protect her always.

One dark night, the princess awoke from a deep slumber and called to her father. But the king did not come. Again she called. Again he did not come.

Then, out of nowhere, arose a fierce storm. Trees began to bend and break. The howling became deafening. Holding onto the sides of her bed, the princess called with all her might, "Father! Come here! I am so frightened!" But the king did not come. She called again, "Father! Where are you?" Still the king did not come. By now the windows were rattling and the walls were buckling.

The princess tried to get out of bed to find her father but the shaking was so violent she couldn't. She pulled the covers over her head and rolled herself into a shivering ball.

The noise was thunderous and glass shattered around her. Gathering all her strength, she peeked out of the covers and saw her possessions sailing past her in all directions, only to crash against the collapsing walls of her bedchamber. She tried to swallow, but her heart pounded wildly in her throat. Nevertheless, the princess shouted once more, "Father!" But The Good King did not come. He did not come.

As the princess wept, her bed began to spin ... slowly at first, then faster and faster. Her covers flew off. She hugged the bedpost but lost her hold and soared through the shattered window. As she sailed into the inky night, the rain and her tears washed together on her face. It was then the princess knew she was going to die ... and she did.

At some point, in a profound way, the dad abandons his daughter by giving up his role of The Good Father. He forsakes her by either inappropriately "turning toward" her (as in some form of abuse), or by "turning away from" her (through detachment of some kind). His healthy father role may be given up deliberately or not. In any event, the princess part of the daughter consequently dies. In the loss there is a shift.

When she awoke, she found herself in a small clearing in a dark forest. The surrounding trees were tall, black, dense, and the earth from which they sprung: dry and cracked. Here and there dead wood was strewn about. The tiny patch of sky above was colorless. Before her lay a small gray pond covered in slimy lily pads. She sat there, lifeless, staring vacantly. When she began to move, she was aware that something was different. Once she could skip and run, but now she only hobbled. She felt awkward in her new skin. "Strange," she croaked. But the newly born frog put her thoughts aside and clumsily slid into the murky ooze of the stagnant water.

Our heroine "awakens" dazed, confused, and numb. She now "stoops" where once she stood proud, "hobbles" where once she ran sure. The shift takes her from fairy tale to nightmare, princess to frog. The incident can seem so shocking that after the initial impact, denial rushes in to protect its victim. Taking it all in at once would be too overwhelming.

It is possible this is not the initial event it appears to be. Very likely other events of an abandoning nature have occurred previously, and that until this point there has been a need and an ability to maintain the fantasy of father as Good King. But suddenly there comes a moment in which illusion or hope collapses ... in which denial can no longer hold. Then, each time reality seeps in, denial soon resurfaces to protect once again.

Eventually, the princess, now a frog, tried to make a place for herself at the pond. There were days she felt competitive and tried to catch more flies than any of the creatures that also lived at the cold water's edge. When she wasn't fighting with them, she helped the others with their problems. Sometimes she felt shy and standoffish; other times she could be quite charming. Periodically she was fidgety or rebellious.

Now the daughter ... The Princess Frog ... doesn't quite know how to be in the world. Her very foundation has been severely shaken. She struggles to re-identify herself by trying out different roles. She feels awkward, uncomfortable in her own skin, and can be very erratic in her behavior. Part of her is shutdown and cut off.

Time passed. Eventually, the frog became restless. Something was wrong. Something was terribly wrong. She looked around at the dark forest she had never dared to enter in all the time she had lived at the pond. The gray leaves on the black trees closest to her began to rustle in the light breeze that whipped up from nowhere. The branches swayed as if bowing to her. Then she heard one especially gnarled tree speak.

"Come. Come into the forest."

"No, no. I'm too frightened!" The frog shrank back and dipped one of her hind feet into the pond.

"Then come when you are ready," said the tree. With that, the wind died down and the trees resumed their silent poses.

The frog began to think more and more about the forest as she became disenchanted and depressed with her life at the pond. Something seemed to be pulling her in the direction of the trees.

I wonder what is in the forest? There is no path. I'll be alone. What if I get lost? What if I never find my way out? What if I am eaten?

She asked the other creatures what they thought she should do. Some said she should go, some said she should stay. The frog thought about it some more.

One day, the frog hobbled toward the gnarled tree. As she did, the wind churned against the tree's branches and its leaves shimmered.

"Why should I come into the forest?" croaked the frog.

"To find what you shall find, to see what you shall see, and to know what you shall know."

"But there is no path."

"You must make your own way," replied the tree. Then it spoke no more.

A deep silence fell over the small clearing, and the frog stared for a very long time at the slimy pond while flies circled lazily overhead in the faint shaft of dull light.

Finally, the frog turned, faced the trees, held her breath, and limped her way into the forest.

At some point, The Princess Frog might begin the healing process. She may enter it willfully as a soldier enters a battle, cautiously or reluctantly as a frightened mouse, or be flung into it like Alice who falls down a rabbit hole. Often a depression caused by a broken love affair will be the catalyst, a divorce, perhaps an anxiety or panic attack, or just a gnawing feeling that something is wrong.

The drive to heal is compelling, yet the need for what is familiar (no matter how uncomfortable or dysfunctional) is also strong. Therefore, the healing process is not entered into lightly. There is usually a struggle going on within the individual.

One part of her says, "I'm scared. I don't want to look at anything. Maybe I can't survive." Another voice says, "There must be something better. I need to take a look so I can go on with my life in a more satisfying way." This part of the daughter is frequently out of the reach of consciousness, yet pushes her to take the step.

Often a mentor inspires or coaxes her to action. At first the daughter may hold back and refuse the call, but at some point, usually when the discomfort becomes too great to tolerate, she will take the risk.

Once inside the woods, the frog felt dwarfed by the endless array of looming trees. She tried to find her way back to the pond in the shadowy light, but couldn't. She thought about moving ahead, or perhaps going left or right. Instead, she sat motionless on the soft, moist soil in that desolate place between forwards, backwards, and sideways.

Entering the process of healing and recovery, the daughter finds she cannot go back to what was. She has crossed over a line, and that experience has changed her. She no longer fits the old mode, yet has not progressed to a new one. She is in limbo.

Sitting there, the frog felt a gentle breeze brush across her webbed feet. She thought she heard the teeniest sound coming from the nearby foliage. Upon inspection, she saw what appeared to be luminous, green grapes lying side-by-side on a leaf. They were eggs. A dark caterpillar was wriggling out of one of them, its front feet grabbing at the newfound air.

Curious as to what else might be in the forest, the frog hobbled on. She began making decisions about where to go and how to get there. Sometimes she followed along a line of trees; on occasion she chose to shuffle among the nettles or pine cones. Now and then she went to the left. To the right. Then straight ahead once more. Periodically, she decided to hurry; every so often she chose to slow down.

When the daughter is on the healing journey, she begins to claim her own authority by making choices about her life. For example, she may decide to enter therapy, go back to school, take a painting class, end an unhealthy relationship, stop asking for other people's advice or opinions, or try on different roles with men. She starts to release herself from old patterns that have kept her stuck.

Along the way, the frog took time to examine a canopy of branches floating above her. From the tree limbs, slender leafy fingers reached out to one another in friendship. She croaked softly and managed to turn up one side of her mouth ever so slightly. This was the closest she had ever gotten to a smile. Remember, she didn't have lips or, for that matter, a tail to wag.

Still looking up, the frog noticed something break the rhythm of the blanket of leaves. Drawing closer, she discovered a large snake wrapped around a low branch; half of its crimson and gold body almost touched the ground. The serpent's argyle-patterned coat glistened on the slender bough. The frog's breath quickened, and she stubbed her front feet as she tumbled to a halt. She swallowed hard, closed her eyes, and hoped the snake hadn't seen her. Frozen to the earth, she held her breath. She knew that, though beautiful, the snake was also dangerous.

It's hard to say how long the frog stood there, close to the snake, with her eyes squeezed shut. *Is it going to bite me? Eat me? Should I wait? Jump away as fast and far as I can?*

She decided to take a peek. She mustered the strength to look up at the snake. It gazed back at her and their eyes became locked in a kind of embrace. The frog began to swoon, but then a strange thing happened. Feeling a sense of power rise in her, she straightened up. Still entranced, the frog slowly turned and hobbled off into a patch of cool undergrowth where she found herself thinking about the snake for a long time.

The wound the daughter suffered by the Father-King left her broken. On the healing journey, she can begin to feel her power. When she does, it is a precarious time, since she doesn't know exactly how to do that. "Power" comes from the French word *pouvoir,* which means "to be able." Feeling her able-ness, or power in life, is a beautiful thing.

But without experience, insight, and maturity, she can easily misuse power and set herself up for danger. For example, the daughter's newfound strength can get her in touch with her anger, which she may spew inappropriately. She can easily slip into a need to control, or become abusive rather than use her power in a constructive way. Dreams involving snakes can appear during this time, since the snake holds attributes of both the able-ness of power and the threat of danger.

Again, the frog moved along in the forest, jumping over fallen trees, ducking under toadstools and fern fronds.

One crisp morning, she heard noises and turned to see a bearded old man chopping wood in a small clearing. Next to him sat a young boy scraping the earth with a twig.

***Wow!* The frog hadn't seen human beings in so long ... not since she had been one herself, living in the palace.**

"Hey! Hello there!" The frog let out her loudest croak. She saw her joy-filled heart pop right through the wall of her chest and jump ahead in the direction of the boy. She caught up with it and breathlessly plopped into his lap.

"Grandfather! A frog!"

"Grab it!" The old man dropped his axe.

The frog gasped and almost swallowed her tongue. She scrambled out from between the boy's legs and began jumping over and around the piles of chopped wood. At times the youngster managed to take hold of the frog's leg, but she was always able to wriggle free.

Finally, the old man cornered her next to a tree and snatched her up. He smacked his lips. "Let's cook it … mmmmm frog legs."

"Nah," said the boy. "Let's string it up and hang it from a tree branch like I done that other time to that there squirrel, 'member?" He fingered the furry hat on his head, and then took some cord out of his pocket.

The two began to argue and the frog felt a shiver sneak its way down from her neck to her webbed feet. She tried to think of a way to free herself, but the old man had a firm grip on her. The more the man and boy argued, the more suffocated the frog felt under the strong fingers surrounding her. Finally, she could endure no more. The image of the snake flashed before her eyes and she remembered the power she had felt in its presence.

"Put me down! You are a cruel old man and a mean, mean boy! Let me go!"

With that, the frog suddenly found herself plunked in the middle of the clearing. She looked around. She was alone … It was magic!

Relieved, she flung back her head and forced out a croak that filled the air. But her giddiness was short-lived when she sensed something behind her. Maybe the nasty boy and man weren't gone after all. Trembling, she turned around

to see her shadow standing behind her. When she hobbled away, it attached itself to her feet and followed her.

On the journey to healing, The Princess Frog at some point may begin to name the shadowy parts of herself ... those fragments, which she has been unaware of or she has rejected.

The Shadow is the part of the daughter that lies in darkness; it must be brought into the light if she is to heal. By embracing its existence as part of her rather than denying it, she opens the possibility of having The Shadow work for her, not against her. (See Appendix A: The Shadow)

The frog meandered for a long time in the forest. Exhausted, she stopped to rest. Closing her eyes, she was carried off into that cloudy place of enveloping slumber. In her dream, a black bird with outstretched wings swept toward her. Panicked, the frog jumped into a hole at the base of a nearby crumbling tree stump. The bird screeched, buried its head in the cavity and tried to bite the frog, which huddled against the side of the hole to escape the scissor-like beak.

The Princess Frog on the healing journey faces obstacles. Her dreams may be filled with grizzly animals, hungry reptiles, stinging insects, clawing birds intent on her destruction. She is chased. She is stalked. She may get bitten. She may become trapped. Her dreams can reflect the injustices inflicted by others in her waking life: her discounting husband, lover, friend or boss. They might mirror her own inner criticisms of herself, which keep her from fulfilling her hopes and dreams, such as: "You're stupid." "You can't get anything right." "You're selfish."

Shaking, the frog awoke to a crackling sound and a faintly unpleasant odor. When the smell became more intense, she realized it was filling her nostrils and choking the air. She had difficulty seeing; she had trouble breathing. As the cloud of smoke momentarily parted, a flaming tree appeared before her. The gray haze rose until it was swallowed up into the tiny patch of sky above. The area surrounding the tree lay charred and parched. The frog tried to hurry across the shriveled earth, but her feet kept getting caught in the hot, dry cracks.

When the wounded Princess Frog is on her journey of recovery, she could find herself stuck in a "dry" state. That is, she might shut down and be unable to cry. Or, she may find herself needing to slow down and make her world smaller in order to cope. She could start cutting back on activities. Feeling the complexities of life, she may seek the comfort of cocooning at home. She might have a need to flee a room because voices or noises, which normally wouldn't have bothered her in the past, can now seem unbearably loud. She may feel claustrophobic in crowds. She is in a struggle to pare things down ... a kind of "drying out" ... to make things more manageable. If she doesn't, she may become overwhelmed and suffer panic or anxiety attacks.

At last, making her way along the thorny nettles, the frog came across a fuzzy, black caterpillar that opened and closed like a jackknife as it inched along the shadowy forest floor. With every step, the fluff on its undulating body sparkled and danced in the faint light. The frog recognized the little caterpillar as the one she had seen emerging from its egg when she had first entered the forest.

"Well, hello again."

The caterpillar looked up. "Hi. Have a nice day." It then folded its way into the blanket of the forest, leaving the frog to sit by herself among the thorns.

The sky suddenly darkened and she found shelter under a small fern just as the gathering clouds spilled their glistening drops. The frog let her mind wander as she stared at the beads of water teetering on the rims of the fronds overhead.

She began to think. She recalled having once been a princess with a wonderful Father-King. She remembered how he had let her down. She thought about how she had become a frog, her dismal life first at the pond, and now in the gloomy forest. She wondered if she would ever find her way to a better place.

Then, as the drops along the edges of the leaves began surrendering to the thirsty ground below, the frog did something different.

She began to feel. She suffered the loss of the wonderful father she had known, and the abandonment, rejection, and betrayal that came as a result. The awkwardness of the life she experienced at the pond, and the loneliness and confusion in the seemingly endless forest now gripped her. Fear overtook her.

With these feelings came a tremendous welling up of tears, and panic swept over her. She had been so afraid she might start to cry. *Oh, no! What if I can't ever stop?*

Too late! She wept so hard, her tears fell to the ground where they became a river, rushing past the neighboring trees. And beyond.

When The Princess Frog begins to get in touch with her feelings of abandonment, rejection, betrayal, loss, and sadness, she cries. She can cry a lot. And sometimes out of nowhere. Never knowing when it's coming or if it will stop, leaves her feeling out of control.

At this point in her journey to recovery, she may have water dreams. Common themes are: drowning, being lost at sea, hanging on to the side of a boat or a piece of driftwood in a storm. This is the stage of "melting" (softening) necessary for her to get unstuck so she can begin to move forward in a new way. Every tear brings her closer to healing.

The frog's eyes stung. She closed them, hoping for rest, and fell into another dream. This time, wild dogs were chasing her, their yellow eyes circling in their sockets. With gnashing teeth nipping at the frog's feet, their hot saliva peppered the frog's back. There could be no escape.

Gripped with terror, she awoke with a jerk.

Nightmarish dreams can continue to plague the daughter as her unconscious mind struggles to deal with and work through her wounding. (See Appendix B: Dreams)

It was then the frog noticed a wavy black line moving just past her feet. Bending forward to investigate, she saw a row of ants scurrying along the forest floor. One especially tiny ant had difficulty keeping up and was getting jostled in the process. It was left behind as the others vanished into the soggy undergrowth ahead. In a frenzy, the ant began to dart every which way.

It ran into the frog.

With one of her webbed feet, the frog scooped up the ant. "What's wrong?"

"I'm scared! I lost my parents. They moved ahead of me in the line and I can't see them anymore. They haven't come back for me." Tears threatened to sneak from the corners of its eyes.

Anger, different from any the frog had felt in the past, grew and grew and grew. It made her eyes bulge even more than usual. Her chest began to heave and her cheeks quivered.

Somewhere along the way, the daughter can experience the most intense form of anger as part of the mourning process: RAGE. Perhaps for the first time, she may feel like railing against life ... the world in general, or perhaps men in particular. Like the flow of tears, feelings of rage can explode in great force as the veil of numbness lifts even more.

The Princess Frog often gets in touch with her anger when she sees others suffering from various forms of abandonment and loss. Eventually, she may begin to feel it in relation to what happened to her. She can come to realize that her strong reaction to pain in others is related to her own wounding, and the empathy ignited in her comes from knowing that pain firsthand.

"Don't worry," said the frog. "I will help you."

She put the tiny ant on her chest next to her heart. Determined to find its parents, she took a long-distance leap in the direction of the vanishing ant line. She discovered the parents talking and laughing with others near a large anthill nestled against the fallen branch of an old tree. When the frog put the small ant down, it scurried to its mother and held on tightly to one of her legs.

The frog, feeling her cheeks turn hot, wondered how her anger could now feel even BIGGER than it did a few minutes ago.

"Look here! Didn't you notice your child was missing? You need to take care of your little ant! It's up to you to protect it and keep it safe. Parents are supposed to watch out for their children because they are too young to do so alone. Good parents don't abandon their little ones!" Sputtering words in her gruffest voice, the frog felt the BIGGEST anger ever!

The parents hung down their heads in shame and magically changed from black ants into blushing red ones. In that moment, the frog wondered if all red ants were really black ants in disguise. Then it occurred to her: might she really still be a princess in disguise?

The frog blinked her way back into the moment, just in time to hear the parents promise to change their ways. Satisfied, the frog picked up the little ant on her webbed foot one last time, and they smiled at each other.

After returning the ant to the arms of its parents, she felt most of her anger float away like a snowy dandelion in the wind. She croaked goodbye to the family as she hobbled ever deeper into the thick, dark woods.

In time the frog came to a narrow break in the trees and saw a slender path winding before her. She couldn't believe her eyes! There, in the crook of the road ahead, she noticed several frogs crouching together under a sign, which read:

GROWTH ROAD
10,000 TEARS TO HEALING

The frog was so excited, she almost stumbled over the webbing on her toes as she jumped as fast as she could to reach the frogs before her. What joy!

"How did you all get here? Does this path lead out of the forest? What does that sign mean?" The words burst forth from the frog's mouth like hot fluffy corn from a popper.

"Slow down! Sit with us and we will answer all your questions," said a grayish-green frog, hopping from under a cluster of rocks.

So the breathless frog plunked herself down and listened. Some, like her, had purposely entered the forest, several jumped in accidentally when they weren't looking, and a number were thrown into it. Quite a few had been there a long time; a handful had arrived only recently. None seemed to know where the path led, or how to escape. And what the sign meant was likewise a mystery to them all.

The frog sat for a long time with her new friends. It was nice to have company. They talked, played leapfrog, and then, one by one, shared their sad tales of loneliness, confusion, and pain long into the night. Their croaks and tears filled the space by the crook in the road as the silent forest slept.

Sometimes The Princess Frog will meet others like her, who have experienced father-wounding. A measure of comfort can be found in the mutual sharing of their pain. But it may not be enough.

Days came and went. After a while the frog grew uneasy. Tired of feeling lost and not knowing who she really was, she wanted to move on and find her way out of the darkness. Was she doomed to be simply a frog lost in the confusion of the forest for all time? Was she ever to be a princess once more? She invited her friends to join her on the path. But no one wanted to go. Some were scared, some were lazy, some would only complain.

The frog held herself back so she could be with her friends. The thought of going on alone was terrifying. And it was hard to leave friends behind. What if she couldn't find new ones?

So the frog stayed for a while until one day she had a dream in which she found a silver string tied to her neck. It dragged her forward along the road away from the others. No matter how hard she tried to dig the backs of her webbed feet into the soil, the glimmering cord kept pulling her until she could no longer see her friends. Finally it spoke to her.

"Invite others to join you on the Growth Road, but hold yourself back for no one."

So, the following morning, the frog bade her friends goodbye, wished them luck, and hopped beyond the bend in the road, wondering what would happen next.

As in the beginning of her journey, the daughter now gathers the courage to separate herself from the pack and venture forth into uncharted territory. Doing so may result in the loss of, or change in, some relationships. Mutual interests can vanish, and values no longer be shared; what once worked, may cease. This idea can be very disturbing and threatening to The Princess Frog who is seeking support and security on her journey.

She must be brave enough to trust that new, healthier relationships will emerge in time as she gets healthier. People of like mental health tend to attract each other. Loyalty and the fear of losing relationships can initially keep The Princess Frog stuck until she decides that nothing will stop her in her quest for growth and healing.

After a few twists and turns, the frog found herself jumping uphill, dodging the brambles at the foot of the trees. But it didn't seem difficult to do. The higher she went, the thinner the air became and she felt lightheaded and peaceful, as if she were floating over the underbrush on tiny winged feet. She remembered feeling wonderful when she stuck up for the little ant and how proud she was that she didn't let anything stop her from moving forward, not even her friends. The frog puffed out her chest and began to sing a happy rhyme in her croaky little voice:

"Look at me!
You can see
Oh how special
I can be!"

Exhibiting her biggest smile to date, the frog was finally hopeful about her journey and the possibility of getting through the forest maze.

At some point, the daughter involved in the healing process, can feel a spiritual shift. Others may call it more of an awakening. It is a time for greater awareness, perspective, and insight. It can seem as if she has been sleeping and now suddenly awakens to a greater realization that she is more than she thought she was—more intelligent? creative? talented? interesting? attractive? etc. She entertains the idea that her dreams, which come from an unconscious part of herself, can be her teachers. She begins to see the dynamics being played out in relationships. This awareness can bring a sense of self-wonder, self-understanding, and self-compassion. She may become conscious of the fact that she could be worth something after all.

As the frog continued up the grade, she was so engrossed in how exhilarated she felt, that she failed to notice another sign partially concealed behind a low hanging tree branch that read:

Caution!
Danger Ahead

Then ... it happened.
Without warning, she dropped

down

down

down

faster and faster ... until a hard surface broke her fall. Blump! She guessed she was in a cave of some sort, but couldn't tell for sure. It was so dark. In fact, she couldn't see. She couldn't see anything at all.

Just when The Princess Frog thinks she's got it all figured out and is on a good path, she can fall. She is suddenly in a dark place: exhausted and bogged down with heavy, often repressed feelings of anger, fear, guilt, resentment, and despair. Something is dying ... and needs to. She is depressed. She may feel as though she is running in quicksand ... in slow motion ... like a movie at the wrong speed. The simplest of tasks can seem overwhelming. She makes her world small, only having the energy for the barest of things that must be done. Her deep, unresolved feelings have caught up with her and anchor her down. All looks gray and bleak, lonely and hopeless. Yet, somehow, in this internal journey into darkness, she finds the strength to move on, moment by moment ...

The frog inched her way along the side of the cave. The uneven wall and rocky floor were damp and icy cold. She shivered. After stumbling around for a while, she realized that she must be in some sort of passageway. She began to feel helpless and alone. More depressed and discouraged than ever, the frog kept going. As she moved forward, she kept repeating, "I will get through this!"

A faint beam of light seeped through the cracks overhead. The frog quickened her pace, encouraged there might be a way out.

Then ... Whoa! She stopped short. She blinked. She blinked again. Her eyeballs grew the size of gumballs as they strained in their sockets.

BEFORE HER LOOMED AN OMINOUS CREATURE.

What it was exactly, was difficult to comprehend since the frog had never seen anything like it. Stringy, matted black hair trailed from exceptionally short legs, keeping the monster's center of gravity close to the ground. Stubby, equally furry arms dangled from the extra wide, squat torso, making the limbs look even more dwarfed. Paw-like bony protrusions engulfed claws that slid in and out with every breath the creature took.

The stocky body itself, unlike the hairy limbs, was covered in large scales, dark and dripping with slime. The vile-smelling, festering ooze smothered the space.

Then, there was the head, which sat in a nest of writhing snakes. The gray skull overwhelmed the body with its massive size. While the torso was low and wide, the head towering above suggested a tall, shapeless blob. Several large red eyes, arranged helter-skelter like darts on a dartboard, peered out from the puckered mass of inky skin. The hole which served as the mouth, revealed a few rotting stumps of ragged teeth. The dappled crimson tongue rolled in and out between them as it danced in concert with the sliding claws, heaving chest and dripping slime.

The frog, her heart racing with terror, squinted in disbelief at the huge image ... at least twenty frogs high and ten frogs wide! *Is this yet another bad dream? Is this nightmare real?*

When the beast saw her, it lumbered forward with a tremendous growl. At first the frog froze, unable to move, her webbed feet stuck fast to the cold, clammy ground below. She felt a pounding behind her eyes. Then, as if by magic, her feet began to move. She leapt every which way— here, there, back and forth—avoiding the fang-like talons and jagged teeth of her attacker.

Quick! Jump! Back down the passageway! But something stronger had crept up within her. It made her stay and confront what lay before her.

I will get through this ... I will get through this ...

The frog faced her foe and soon realized she was quite good at outmaneuvering it. While she could move quickly, her short-legged aggressor was slow and clumsy. She also noticed that the monster was striking with only one of its paws; the other kept vigil over its heart.

She had a hunch. *This may not be the monster I think it is. I wonder what its paw might be protecting.*

Scared but determined, she began taunting the creature by jumping up and down, approaching ever closer in a zigzag fashion. If the frog could only get the monster to remove the other bony paw from the area of its heart, her plan might work. As luck would have it, the beast, increasingly infuriated by the frog's ability to avoid getting caught, soon started swiping at her with both paws.

The frog had been able to avoid getting hurt so far, but the stench from the putrid slime was close to overwhelming. She knew if she didn't do something soon, the monster would overtake her. Seizing the opportunity, the frog swallowed hard, hunkered down and pushed off the ground with all her might. It was the biggest leap she'd ever taken.

As she flew at the creature, she managed to jump between its stubby outstretched arms, landing smack on its heart with an eerie thud that echoed through the passageway. The frog hopped off as the monster cried out in thunderous screams. The beast ricocheted off the protruding walls of the freezing passageway as it melted to the ground. The cave shook violently and rocks cascaded down its sides, while the frog quickly found shelter under the protection of a small bulge in the wall. She looked back just in time to see the creature's staring red eyes roll back into its head and disappear, leaving large, gaping cavities for the snakes to explore before slithering into the hidden cracks of the damp, oh-so-cold cave.

In order for transformation to take place, some things must die. In the daughter, they are her illusions, weaknesses, and dysfunctional roles. She must be willing to "slay the dragon" of her oppression … that which keeps her stunted as a human being. Fighting for transformation takes courage. It is heroic. The task is great; the reward greater. Often forgiving, grieving, and confronting one's Shadow, are the means to finding the way out of the darkness into the light.

The frog inched her way past the body of the sprawling beast and hobbled further down the cave, scraping the slimy ooze off her webby feet as she went.

She thought about what had happened. Unlike some of her dreams in which she was helpless, the frog had been able in a real life situation to take charge and save herself. New feelings of pride and a sense of power filled her. Chest inflated like a balloon, her webbed feet barely touched the ground.

Floating down the corridor in the dim light, the frog failed to notice the passageway had gotten narrower and narrower. Before she knew it, she found herself lodged between the jagged walls, unable to move in any direction. She was stuck!

Quietly, the frog waited …
And she waited …
Then she waited some more.

At some point along the way, The Princess Frog will come to a standstill. The road to growth and healing is not like walking up a ladder … step by step. It is more like attempting to climb a mountain. Sometimes she'll move forward; sometimes she'll fall back; other times she'll reach a plateau … come to an impasse. This is a critical time for her. She must not panic. She needs to be careful not to act out of fear; revive old feelings of self-doubt; define herself as a victim by blaming others; act on suicidal thoughts; slip back into familiar, catastrophic patterns (such as self-cutting, abusing drugs or alcohol, engaging in reckless sex, resurrecting eating disorders, tolerating destructive relationships).

Not compromising herself or her principles, and allowing a difficult or painful situation to resolve itself, can be hard. Hope, patience and trust are required. Instead of seeing herself as "stuck," she must assume things will change, either by circumstance or by her own doing. Prayer and/or meditation can be helpful at this time.

The frog was wedged for quite a while between the walls.
Soon she fell asleep and began to dream about the sea.
Beautiful rainbow-colored fish swam between dense rocks
along the ocean floor. The fish appeared fat and round,
until they turned to face her. As they did, she could see they

were actually thin as paper. Consequently, they could move between the rocks easily.

The frog awoke from her dream chuckling. She stared at the craggy rocks on either side of her and sucked in as hard as she could till she, herself, looked like a pancake. Easily sliding out from the crevice with a satisfied croak, the frog left the narrow space behind her and made her way back up the passageway in hopes of finding another way out of the cave.

Along the road to growth and healing, there may be coincidences of significance. For example, if The Princess Frog is struggling with a bad relationship and cannot make the decision to leave, she might have a dream in which she escapes or walks away from danger or confusion. Perhaps she happens upon some information from an outside source that sheds bad light on her partner, spurring her to move on. Someone may suggest an obscure book or movie, which coincides with her struggle, and offers a solution. She can take these events as "signs" and choose to act on them as guides for behavior. What is noteworthy is that these "meaningful coincidences" (what Carl Jung called "synchronicity") cannot be explained through cause and effect; they occur simultaneously. This is reminiscent of the old saying: "When the student is ready, the teacher will appear." This speaks to the notion of learning to stay open and receptive to that, which may provide insight and help.

She stumbled upon a corridor she had missed earlier in her haste to get away from the reeking creature's corpse. As she entered the passageway, she noticed just ahead, a thin stream of light punching it's way through the yawning abyss. Excited, the frog jumped as fast as she could, her heart racing in anticipation. When she caught up to the sliver of a crack in the rocky wall, she felt herself bathed in warm light. She scrambled to look through the slit. As her eyes adjusted to the pale yellow sunlight, she smiled so broadly, the two ends of her mouth almost met at the back of her head.

Peeking through the crack, she could make out some slender brown trees at the foot of a slope just outside the cave. No longer a crowded forest, the trees were sparser, giving the soft sunbeams room to flicker between the leaves and cast long stretches of light onto the soil below.

The frog flung herself against the crack in the wall and, with a great deal of stretching and twisting, was able to get her head through. She then closed her eyes and sucked in her body as she had done before. After many painstaking attempts, the frog slipped through the narrow opening. She spilled onto the soft earth below, landing on her belly.

"I knew I could get through this!" she croaked.

The frog rubbed her bruised body, then sat down for a moment to rest. She looked up and noticed something moving on one of several twigs that grew above the crack outside the cave. A butterfly had just emerged from its dangling cocoon and was unfolding its wings to allow them to dry in the sunshine. The frog and the butterfly

looked at one another. Each had come struggling out of the dark into the light.

When The Princess Frog first comes out of the darkness, she feels shaky. Sometimes she experiences a renewal of her pain, but if she endures it a little longer, she will come through it.

In time, the world appears somewhat different: less overwhelming, less threatening. She feels changed as well: a survivor, stronger, more assured, with a deeper sense of who she is. Like a caterpillar emerging as a butterfly from a cocoon, the daughter is transforming from frog into something new.

The frog admired the butterfly's colorful wings with black markings.

"Hello," said the butterfly. "It's been a while since last we spoke in the deep forest."

Now remembering the furry, black caterpillar, the frog said, "Yes, and so much has happened to me since then. But I see you have changed as well."

" I have indeed!" laughed the butterfly. It's a wonder you recognize me."

After chatting for a time, the frog waved goodbye and limped down the slope as fast as her still-sore frog legs could carry her, anxious to get as far away from the dark cave as possible.

The butterfly followed along, then winked at her as it flitted away into the trees beyond.

The frog approached the bottom of the hill … and gasped.

In the sun-flecked mist before her, several cottages floated down from the sky and came to rest in the soil around the scattered trees ahead. The frog tripped over her feet and landed on her chin as she counted six houses, each different from the next. And every one looked so big to so small a frog.

What do I do? I'm scared to see what I might find behind those doors. She squatted and dug her webbed feet into the cool earth to consider the matter.

It was all so strange. She was still shaken from having just come out of the darkness. But in time the shafts of sunlight, which warmed her back and now illuminated the forest, made her feel somehow more confident. Taking a deep breath, she jumped up the path to the first cottage: a dirty, gray abode punctuated with black trim.

Before she could knock, the door flew open with a loud BANG! which echoed throughout the forest.

A judge, his forehead splashed with v-shaped ruts, shook his gavel at her while his black robes rippled with each word. "What do YOU want, you stupid frog?"

The frog hung her head.

"Who are you anyhow? You're NOBODY! You're WORTHLESS!" spat The Judge.

The frog sank lower and lower until she was spread flat on the stoop.

The Judge bent over the frog, coming closer and closer to her head with his gavel. "You're good for nothing! You ARE nothing!"

The frog felt defeated. The Judge obviously knew her well; she couldn't fool him. Truly, she was nothing but a mere frog. Had she been something special ... prettier, smarter, more interesting or charming ... her father would never have forsaken her. She deserved to be unloved. The frog closed her eyes and wished she could disappear.

Satisfied, The Judge retreated into his house with a cackle and slammed the door.

The Princess Frog can easily slip back into despair and self-doubt when confronted by the part of herself that judges and criticizes her harshly. Whenever the daughter successfully comes through any kind of challenge and gains a sense of power and self-esteem, The Judge often cuts her down. And like a newborn foal that finally comes to stand on its wobbly legs, The Princess Frog can easily be knocked over.

It is when the daughter begins to see herself in a favorable light ... as survivor rather than victim ... that an internal struggle may occur. Empowered and elated on the one hand, wondering: "Who am I?" on the other, she can become confused and disoriented. She might feel like a fraud. The Judge takes advantage of The Princess Frog's struggle, undermining her self-worth by keeping her guilty, vulnerable, shameful and fearful. And stuck.

The Judge is often the manifestation of a critical parent the daughter had encountered growing up, who led her to believe that she was a failure or disappointment because she was no good or not good enough. (See Appendix C: The Judge)

Scarcely a moment passed, when the frog heard the rich, sweet-sounding voice of a woman calling to her.

The frog scraped herself up off the stoop and looked around. Filling the doorway of the nearby second cottage, stood a crone. The old woman's white gown held all the colors of the rainbow, and matched the paint on her house. She had the brightest eyes the frog had ever seen. And when she opened her mouth to speak, the forest stilled.

"Don't listen to the critical Judge. You DO have value. Remember how you helped the lost little ant? The way the frogs wanted you to be their friend? How the butterfly remembered you and seemed to enjoy talking to you? And think of what you have survived: a storm, a fire, a monster. A lot of pain. Surely your caring heart, your courage, your likeability means you are something after all."

"Who are you?"

"I am The Wise Woman."

"Whatever do you mean?"

"I see things you can't see. I see the bigger picture and share with you what is real. The Judge will do anything and everything to tear you down and make you doubt yourself. I'm here to guide you, nurture you, and tell you what is true."

Besides wisdom, The Wise Woman part of the daughter carries wholeness, balance, peace and hope. She has the vast perspective of a great soaring bird, unlike the small frog that sees only a narrow world before her. The wisdom of The Wise Woman is born both from the hard knocks of life experience and from the internal place of knowingness, which the daughter has available to her if she dares to listen. When we hear wisdom, we recognize it. As The Princess Frog dips into that loving internal well, she is free to move toward a higher place, where clear vision and self-acceptance reside.

The daughter can strengthen her Wise Woman by believing in her existence and trusting her good counsel.

"But I think The Judge must be right", said the frog, lowering her head. "I must have done something terribly wrong or been very bad, for my father not to have come when I called him. I must be to blame."

The Wise Woman responded gently, "Isn't it possible that what happened between you and your father was not your fault? That what he did had nothing to do with you?"

The frog wiped away the tears that had begun collecting around her eyes. She attempted to concentrate on this new idea, but as hard as she tried, it kept slipping away from her. The thought seemed just out of reach … like a gauzy light in the fog.

The Wise Woman waited, knowing how important it was for the frog to have the space and time to make sense of this new idea.

"But how could I not be to blame?" croaked the frog, finally. Her eyes met those of The Wise Woman.

"Because you were a child doing what comes naturally. You were scared and needed your father. You called to him because that is what children do, especially when they get frightened. How else should a child act? Should we blame a child for being a child?"

The frog straightened up. "I never thought about it like that."

Typically, the daughter blames herself when her father drops the ball. Partly it is because she is young and doesn't have the whole picture. It is also due to the fact that she, like all children, is self-centered and sees everything in relation to herself. A father is supposed to be in charge; after all, he is god-like to his daughter. As ripping as it is for her to sacrifice herself by taking blame for his actions, it can be nothing compared to the most scary and unbearable idea ... one she can't face: "If my father doesn't know what he is doing or if he doesn't care, how will I survive?"

The door to The Judge's house flung open so violently then, that it tore loose from its hinges. "Don't listen to HER! She's an idiot! You know you're BAD, and nothing she tells you can change that!"

The Wise Woman turned and pointed at The Judge. "Hush, little man." As she lowered her hand, he shrunk in size until he was no bigger than a gnat. Then she snapped her fingers and he vanished.

The frog jumped three frogs high. "Whoa! Where did he go?" She peered into the darkness of The Judge's gray house.

"Oh, he'll likely be back. As long as folks continue to listen to him, he'll keep showing up. The trick is to remember to put him in his place. And he's only as powerful as people allow him to be."

The frog let out a long sigh. "Whew! That is comforting to know." Her skin, which had been crinkling from fear and shame, settled down and embraced her body once more. *This woman is smart and powerful. Maybe she will help me find my way out of the forest.*

As if reading the frog's mind, the knowing crone said, "Before you can move forward, you must visit the rest of the houses. Shall I come with you?"

Nodding, the frog hopped along beside her as they approached the third cottage. Out of the corner of her eye, the frog caught sight of The Judge lurking behind a tree. *If he says anything, I'll be ready for him.*

The house was tiny and very pink. Plopped on the windowsill, missing a shoe was a doll with yellow braids and faded red ribbons. The door opened, and a young princess peeked out ... the very same one the frog had been so long ago when she lived in the castle with her father. She was dressed in a wispy lavender gown covered with tiny stars that twinkled among the folds. Atop her head sat a small silver tiara encrusted with rubies. Her smile seemed to illuminate her face.

"Where have you been? I have been waiting for you to find me for so long." The princess stretched out her arms in welcome.

The frog froze. She stared in amazement. *What a scrawny, disgusting little runt.*

There comes a time for the daughter to address her Inner Child, if she is ever to heal. (See Appendix D: The Inner Child)

The Judge, shrieking and shaking his gavel, snuck up behind the frog. His heavy black robe flared and shook so hard, it almost knocked her off the stoop.

"That's right. That's RIGHT! She's REPULSIVE, isn't she? Yech! And so UNLOVABLE! So UGLY!"

The frog fell into a trance. The tiara on the girl's head slipped and lay dangling over her ear as a big teardrop rushed down her cheek to rest at the base of her neck. The next one missed altogether and puddled onto the frog's nose. But the frog didn't notice.

The Wise Woman, using her power of wisdom and truth in the face of ignorance, dismissed The Judge yet again. This time she ordered him to leave the forest, and he evaporated immediately. But it was more difficult to detach the frog from her trance.

She appealed to the frog. "Look at this young girl. See how small and dear she is."

The frog was unmoved.

"Look at her tears."

Still the frog was unmoved. She could be kind to everyone else but not to The Child.

The Wise Woman knelt down, stroked the frog's back and stared into her eyes. "You must find a way to accept this girl or she will stay wounded and neither of you will ever heal."

Something stirred in the frog and, for the first time, she really focused on the princess. The frog saw that The Child seemed lost and frightened ... feelings she, herself, knew so well.

The spell was broken! The frog hugged the little one who then snuggled against her, feeling safe at last.

"I want you to know that I see the real you now," croaked the frog.

The Child's lip, which had been trembling, came to rest in a deep sigh. The frog felt touched. She straightened the tiara on the girl's head. "Don't worry. You won't be alone any more. Come with me ... I'll take care of you."

The daughter cannot go back to being Daddy's Little Princess. However, she can reclaim a piece of that special-ness she felt before the father-wounding. Though no one human being is truly more significant than another, it is important for each of us to feel, or have felt, special to someone at some point in life, most especially in childhood when the ego is fragile and a sense of esteem has the potential to develop.

How can the daughter take back the special feeling of the princess she remembers being? By deciding to give herself the Royal Treatment. For example, she may indulge in a new wardrobe, get a facial, buy herself some flowers, or lounge in a bubble bath. By pampering herself, she can come to realize that her sense of special-ness is not lost after all.

There can be a hurdle to this process, however. Often the biggest one for The Princess Frog is to find compassion for her wounded Inner Child. Through father-wounding, she may come to see that part of herself as flawed, shameful, and disgusting. What was once done to her, she now does to herself. That spell must be broken in order for self-compassion to unfold. (See Appendix E: Trance States)

The frog, The Child, and The Wise Woman turned to face the fourth cottage. They all were pleased to note that The Judge was nowhere in sight.

This house stood surrounded by several trees dressed in polka dot ribbons. It had a whimsical look about it: a bent chimney and wavy walls covered in turquoise paint. The frog knocked on the door and a girl appeared. She resembled The Child, though older ... more like a teenager. She had on a filmy, flowery dress and wore a dreamy look on her face. She seemed surprised to find three strangers at her doorstep.

"Oh! I thought you might be my handsome, charming prince come to carry me off. Until he shows up, I guess I'll just have to break a few more hearts. I'm quite irresistible as you can see." She fluttered her long, thick eyelashes and began dancing around the room as she hummed a merry tune.

"Who are you?" said the frog.

"Me? Oh, I'm The Maiden ... can't you tell? Say, aren't men just wonderful?" She giggled and continued to leap about.

The Wise Woman suggested to the frog that they invite the teen to come along with them. "The Maiden is delightful, but so naïve, she could get into trouble," she explained. The frog agreed.

"Excuse me, dear, would you like to come with us?"

The Maiden, excited to think about all the men she could meet, smiled her dreamy smile and, without a word, waltzed out of her house and led the way to the next cottage.

It is important for The Princess Frog to be aware of The Maiden portion of herself, which is idealistic, innocent, shy, or flirtatious. This is the part of her that dreams of romance and drama.

A daughter who has been betrayed or abandoned by her father can be drawn into The Maiden role when relating to the opposite sex. She may easily fall in love, idealize men, and fantasize about romantic interludes. The problem is that the adolescent naiveté of The Maiden can act as a blind spot to the daughter by putting her into difficult—even dangerous—situations.

Early father-daughter trauma creates in The Princess Frog a Maiden who is shortsighted and ill equipped for the nuances and reality of the bigger world. It is as if part of the clock of life has stopped in the daughter at an early age ... often close to when the trauma occurred. Therefore, she can mistake cues from men by misinterpreting their behavior: the "good guys" can seem boring, and the "bad guys" can seem exciting. She can endlessly seek a father figure, or keep a distance from men in general.

Although The Princess Frog must accept The Maiden's existence and acknowledge her struggle, she must not allow that part of her to be in charge. Unless a more rational, mature part of herself such as The Wise Woman is present, the daughter can set herself up for the pain of disappointment, misjudgment, and abandonment with respect to men.

And re-wound herself time and time again.

The frog, The Child, and The Wise Woman caught up with The Maiden at the fifth house, which was painted the same shade of the "GO!" green you find on a traffic light. The frog knocked and this time a man answered with a clock in one hand, a hammer in the other, and several more tools in his belt. The muscles on his body rippled as he moved.

"Hey ... what's up?" He blew a mop of sandy hair out of his eyes.

"Who are you?" said the frog.

"I'm The Man ... don't want to be rude, but I'm kind of busy ... you see, I committed myself to do this here job ... well, there have been all kinds of problems, but I'm determined to finish what I started ... always do ... matter of fact, I think I'm pretty close to getting it done ... (he looked at his clock) ... maybe another ten, fifteen minutes should do it ... how can I help you?"

All human beings have both masculine and feminine energy. Each provides gifts. When these gifts come together effectively, they bring wholeness, balance and peace.

The feminine: is relationship-oriented; distributes information in a soft, non-threatening way; is open to receiving; is complex rather than simple (note woman-to-woman relationships); is somewhat passive; nurtures others; is safely approachable. Like a smorgasbord in which everything from soup to dessert can be seen all at one time, the feminine is aware of and can address several things at once.

While the feminine part is more internally or quietly directed, the masculine piece is more about taking charge. It's about making its presence known, rather than fading into the background. The masculine: deals with asserting oneself; is ready to express and fight for its beliefs; is simple and basic rather than complex: nothing frilly, nothing hidden. It is goal-oriented: seeking heroism by fixing and solving problems; it creates structure and boundaries. If the feminine is like a smorgasbord, the masculine is like a TV set: it focuses on one channel at a time. (See Appendix F: Using Masculine and Feminine Energy Effectively)

The Wise Woman suggested The Man join their group when his job was done. "We could use a fellow like you with drive and focus to help us get through the forest."

The Man put down the clock and hammer. "Well, now, Ma'am, you got yourself a deal. You can count on me." He hooked his thumbs into his belt.

"Splendid. Come meet us in front of the house next door when you're ready."

"Will do."

The Maiden, who had been having trouble keeping quiet all this time, could stand it no more. "Now, don't you be late!" She blushed and batted her eyelashes extra hard.

She, the frog, The Wise Woman, and The Child, all made their way to the sixth cottage. It was the last cottage. While waiting, they sat on an old fallen tree and looked at what was, by far, the largest and the grandest of the houses. It was painted a royal blue mixed with tiny flecks of gold, which glistened in the sun.

When The Man met up with them, they all marched to the door together. The frog knocked. The door opened and there sat her father, the king, on a gilded throne. The frog gasped. The Child hid behind The Wise Woman, and The Maiden tiptoed to the rear of the group next to The Man.

The frog, heart thumping, faced her father. Her feet wobbled on the slick floor.

Neither spoke.

She stared at him for a long time until a large chunk of the king's crown fell off his head and crashed to the floor. The frog looked down at the broken pieces at her father's feet, and then at the remaining fragment on his head. Her father didn't move or make a sound; his eyes stayed glued to the shard-strewn floor. The frog realized in that moment that her father was less a king than a man.

After a time she felt her feet grow strong beneath her. She swallowed hard and heard herself say, "What you did to me wasn't okay."

With that, she turned on her webbed feet and hopped out of the cottage into the soft sunlight. Silently, the others followed.

"And who do you think YOU are, treating your FATHER that way?" shrieked The Judge, as he emerged from the nearby fallen tree.

But the frog was in no mood. "Begone!" she said.

And so he was.

Facing the father in order to go on with her life in a more healthy way, is one of the biggest challenges for The Princess Frog. This may be done directly, by letter, in fantasy, dreams, through therapy, or relationships with other men. (See Appendix G: Confronting The Father)

The frog looked back at all six cottages. She felt different somehow. Her movements were less wobbly, less jerky. Her voice, less croaky. And she noticed her fellow travelers seemed smaller and shorter than before.

She turned to The Wise Woman. "Have I grown?"

"Yes, and I'm proud of you."

"You are?"

"Absolutely. It takes a lot of courage to do all the things you have done. You have fought for yourself, faced what needed to be faced, and still you have been kind to others along the way. You have grown and will continue to do so."

The frog smiled. The kind that stretched back so far behind her head, that the two ends almost touched.

"That's a pretty big smile on your face. Tell me how you feel about all you have accomplished."

The frog stuck out her chest. "I'm very proud of myself, too. I had no idea I could feel this strong and this hopeful." She smiled again and hugged herself so hard, she toppled over onto the ground and laughed. When she got all the giggles out, she grew quiet and closed her eyes.

"Wise Woman?"

"Yes? I'm here."

"I've been thinking. Remember you told me that I could move on after visiting all the houses?"

"Yes."

"Well, now that I've done that, how do I get out of the forest?"

"You need to follow your heart, your intuition, and your common sense. You also need to push yourself through any discomfort along the way. Don't give up. That's how to get to the other side."

"I'm not sure I know what all that means."

"You will. And you don't have to do this alone. We will all help you if you let us. The Child and the Maiden will lead you with their hearts, I will inspire your intuition and common sense, and The Man will make sure you forge ahead and complete the journey. Even The Judge can serve you by challenging you to hold on to the self esteem you now have."

"Will you all stay with me after I get out of the forest?"

"We will always be with you. But it is up to you to remember us."

Being familiar with her parts, gives The Princess Frog the opportunity to be more pro-active in her healing. With awareness, comes power, and with power comes growth.

Somewhere between yesterday and tomorrow, the six cottages disappeared in the morning mist. Erupting clumps of grass and a riot of colorful flowers grew in their stead. Though The Man was anxious to move forward, The Wise Woman said it was time to stop for a while and sort out a few things. So they all came to rest among the blossoms under the leafy umbrella of the forest. Only The Judge seemed to be missing ... though we knew better.

The frog hopped into the lap of The Wise Woman and soon drifted into a dream ... .

She was a princess once again in the palace, laughing as she ran down the grand hallways with her father, the king. But a sudden storm came up, enveloping the castle in total darkness, and she became separated from him. Though she called to her father, he didn't respond. The wind then pulled her from the castle and dropped her into a gloomy marsh in a thick forest. Looking into a pool of gray water, she saw an insignificant frog blankly staring back at her.

The frog stirred in her sleep. Her eyelids danced in her otherwise motionless face. The dream whipped into a frenzy. The frog now found herself in the deep forest where creatures—some friendly, some terrifying—chased after

her. Fire and smoke danced in the background, heating her skin and blinding her sight. Not knowing where to go, she ran every which way among the trees. Finally a grotesque monster grabbed her and drew her towards him. But before he could devour her, POOF! ... the frog ballooned in size as the monster turned into a potato bug, curled up into a ball, and rolled away into the nearby underbrush.

There are times along the way, in which the daughter must stop and absorb what has happened to her, or she will become too overwhelmed. Through various means such as dreams, writing (journaling, poetry), movement (interpretive dance, yoga), meditation, and therapy, she is able to better cope with the impact the journey has made on her so far.

Heart pounding, the frog awoke to find part of her still in The Wise Woman's lap, though barely. In fact, her legs were sprawling onto the soft earth and her eyes were now level with The Wise Woman's collarbone.

"Are you shrinking?" said the frog, not recognizing her own voice. (There was, after all, no croak in it.) This sent a shiver up her backside.

The Wise Woman smiled. "The only way I can shrink is if you let me. It is you who are growing very quickly now."

"Is that why I feel so scared?"

"Change is scary. It was frightening to stop being the princess you were, but it's also frightening to grow into something else."

"So I won't ever go back to being a princess again?"

"No."

The frog felt a sudden sadness. "But what's to become of me?"

"That part of the journey you have yet to create. Trust me. We'll stay in this place for a while so you can get used to these new ideas and changes. In the meantime, you must be patient a little longer."

The frog took a deep breath, closed her eyes and thought about how far she had come. The Child busied herself picking flowers while The Maiden glided among the shrubbery humming a merry tune. The Judge scowled in a tree overhead. But The Man squirmed a bit. After all, it wasn't in his nature to be patient.

Minutes, hours, or days passed ... perhaps months. Who can say? In that time, the frog continued to change. She grew so much, that were she threatened now by that old monster who had lived in the cave, she could merely knock it over with a sigh and a tickle. Of course, there were times when The Judge would sneak up on the frog and drag her heart down with his shaming ways. Then she would shrink back to her lowly beginnings, limp under the closest array of ferns and rest her head on the ground. But that was happening less and less, as were the scary dreams of her past life.

Something else changed as well. The frog found her voice. Her croak, which had long disappeared, was replaced with an increasingly confident and pleasing sound ... strong, yet soft at the same time.

And when she moved, there was nary a hobble, nary a jerk to her stride. (Especially noteworthy since she now walked only on her hind legs!)

One particularly delicious day, when the leaves in the forest hung uncommonly verdant on the branches and the vibrant flowers below lay open to the shafts of sunlight above, The Wise Woman called everyone together. Even The Judge was invited. He grumbled at first, and then sat down on a red and white toadstool a distance from the others.

Meanwhile, the frog sat as close to The Wise Woman as possible without squashing her. The Child climbed into the frog's lap while The Maiden inched her way towards The Man who was too focused on his watch to notice. The Wise Woman cleared her throat and began.

"I'd like to tell you a story about all of us." She pulled a small leather book from her front pocket, and read:

"Somewhere far away—yet oh-so-near—there was a boat dressed in a shade of green as pale as the wisp of a leaf at sunrise. If you looked carefully, past the many chips on its surface, you could barely see the word 'frog' written on each side of the boat. In the beginning, both paint and writing were quite conspicuous, but over time they had gradually faded."

Everyone looked up at the frog who shuffled her feet and kept her eyes on the ground.

"For a long time, the boat had been adrift, at the mercy of the water and weather. Getting constantly tossed about in the sea, it felt lost, helpless and empty."

The frog swallowed hard.

"But at some point, the boat became aware that it wasn't alone after all. It discovered that inside were a former princess—The Child—who had been wounded, the dreamy Maiden who focused on men, The Wise Woman who had vision, The Man who took care of business, and The Judge who snuck back no matter how many times he was thrown overboard.

"Because of these parts that lived within it, the boat didn't feel quite so lonely anymore. Still, the fact that its paint was both fading and peeling, and its shell was beginning to crumble, made the boat aware it was indeed changing. But into what? As miserable as life had been, at least that life was familiar. It was scary to think about becoming something else."

Tears like soap bubbles blown through a wand gushed from the frog's eyes. She was reminded of that time so long ago near the beginning of her journey, when she first entered the forest and didn't know which way to go. She found herself in that place again between forwards, backwards, and sideways.

The Wise Woman patiently waited until the frog's tears ceased to flow. Then she continued with her story.

"Besides changing, the boat had to deal with other problems. Those living inside of her were in a constant struggle for control. Each wanted to be captain of the boat. It seemed that in the beginning, everyone was trying to grab the steering wheel. All except The Wise Woman who was very small in those days and was constantly pushed aside. But she began to grow in time and one day asked them all who they thought should steer the boat most of the time."

The Wise Woman closed the book.

"So, what happened next?" said the frog.

The Wise Woman smiled. "I don't know. The story needs an ending. Who do you think should steer the boat?"

The Child, who had been listening very intently, stood up. "Me! Me! I'd want to drive!" She waved her hands like it was Sunday morning in church.

The Maiden looked up through her eyelashes. "No, me, silly!"

"I could do it! I can fix problems. I can take charge and work quickly." The Man adjusted his tool belt.

"I'm obviously the only one here who would know how to do it! The rest of you are WORTHLESS, INCOMPETENT NOBODIES!" shrieked The Judge. He spun around on his toadstool and turned his back on the group.

The Wise Woman laid a finger alongside her temple. "Let's think about this. Everyone wants to be in charge sometimes. The question is, who would be most likely to keep the boat in balance? Who would stay the steady course, give up the helm only when it was safe, practical or logical to do so? Let's consider the possibilities.

"If The Child steers, the boat could capsize because children are naïve and inexperienced. But a child could have a turn and some fun if a competent person was right there to grab the wheel if necessary.

"Same with The Maiden. If she drives the boat, it could run aground because maidens are gullible and easily distracted. She needs someone there to watch out for her.

"If The Man takes over, the boat could run well most of the time, but other times it might move too quickly. Under certain circumstances, slowing down or even stopping might require a different sort of captain.

"And if The Judge is in charge of the boat, it will definitely sink, and we can't have that!"

The frog sat up straight. "What if The Wise Woman steered the boat? She could let The Child or The Maiden have turns when it was safe enough and could decide when it was best for The Man to take over. She would do a great job of keeping The Judge either off the boat or making sure he would take a backseat."

So, they took a vote and it was agreed (except, of course, by The Judge), that The Wise Woman should be the captain of the crew.

Attending to one's internal components can be an effective exercise. (See Appendix H: Acknowledging One's Parts)

The Wise Woman closed her eyes and nodded. "So, we've written an end to the story of the boat."

"The End? What do you mean?" The frog shot up, sending The Child, who had fallen asleep in her lap, tumbling so fast into the far-off toadstool that its top flew off, throwing it and The Judge to the ground with a thud.

The Judge shook his fist at the frog and grumbled, "@$#%$*&!"

But the frog had something more important on her mind: her life. "What do you mean?" she said to The Wise Woman, this time in a whisper.

"Don't be afraid. You now have everything it takes to move forward to a new chapter. The time has come for you to leave the forest and claim a place for yourself at the banquet of life. Come with me."

The frog, as she followed The Wise Woman, couldn't tell if she was scared or excited. Both emotions felt the same to her, so she decided to be excited.

The others watched for a while, and then caught up. As they walked, fewer and fewer trees dotted the landscape. No thick undergrowth covered the ground ... just a light wash of grass. Sunlight fell easily between pale leafy trees and struck the ground in wide patches. The frog could see farther than before.

When things come together for The Princess Frog ... when she can see the big picture of what happened to her with respect to her father ... she understands that it has nothing to do with her own value. She is now freed from the stranglehold that father-wounding has had on her life. She has the confidence and the tools to deal with the issue when old feelings resurface, which they will. She was wounded. Nothing can erase it. But, the old feelings of despair, loneliness, and confusion will continue to lessen over time. Now she can treat herself with the respect she deserves, seek and demand healthier relationships, and keep her Judge in check. (See Appendix I: Symbols of Wounding and Healing)

Heartened, she took the lead and began to hurry along, as if pulled by an imaginary thread. With each step, she could feel herself growing taller. So tall, in fact, that she soon lost sight of the others.

In the distance she noticed something large and shiny leaning against a tree. Sunbeams struck it, shooting slivers of light towards her. She hurried faster. When she approached the glistening object, she realized it was a mirror. She turned to face it, and saw her reflection.

A woman looked back at her.

The woman wore a flowing white top with matching pants, which billowed in the soft breeze. She looked a bit like the princess she had been so long ago, only older, more mature. She carried a knowingness about her. An air of calmness. A centeredness.

A golden locket and chain dangled from the side of the mirror. The woman opened it and saw The Child, The Maiden, The Man, and The Wise Woman sitting in a circle around a very green frog. They all smiled when they saw her. (The Judge must have been recently put in his place, for he was scowling most ferociously in the background and was decidedly even tinier than the others.) The woman smiled back, closed the locket and slipped it over her head. She looked once again in the mirror. It was then she saw the necklace begin to slowly disappear into a place within her, close to her heart, where it resides to this day.

Turning, the woman continued to walk through the remaining scattered trees.

A round, green meadow lay in the clearing ahead. Above, the large radiant sun beckoned to her. As she neared the open area, several white doves brushed past her and flew into the open space. It was then her friend, the colorful butterfly with black markings appeared and landed on the woman's hand. It greeted her by opening and closing its beautiful wings.

The woman placed the butterfly on her shoulder. She smiled and gave herself a hug, as she walked toward the warm, golden sun.

She lived happily ever after.

Happily ever after?

Well, no, not exactly. That's the stuff of fairy tales. Instead, The Princess Frog embraces her Wise Woman, cherishes her journey, and lives a more balanced, satisfying life filled with a greater sense of peace and wholeness.

But what exactly is wholeness? And how does The Princess Frog find peace with respect to the experience of losing her Good Father? How can she ever find a true resolution?

That is something she strives to achieve in the final stage of her journey. For the daughter, it is true that her father treated her like a princess at one time—that he had "kingly" qualities (kind, attentive, protective, safe, etc.). But the opposite is also true—that he purposely or not, acted "un-kingly" (negligent, insensitive, unboundaried, absent, inappropriate, etc.) by failing to continue in his Good Father role.

The reconciling of opposites—that **both are true**— is one of the ways wholeness may be found. Being able to acknowledge conflicting traits or truths about a person or situation is the challenge. It is not "either-or;" it is "this AND this." To be able to say, "He was a good father AND ALSO not a good father." "I love him AND I don't love him." Acknowledging the all-encompassing truth of things. These are moments of wholeness.

Because we humans are always in flux and can change our feelings and moods, being whole can be fleeting. But with enough consciousness and practice, a greater sense of contentment and wholeness can be found. Reconciling opposites; working with one's Shadow, Judge, Inner Child, dreams, trance states, various parts; or confronting the father ... all potentially bring the daughter closer to integration, balance, peace, and a sense of completeness.

Some Princess Frogs reach a place of forgiveness; others do not. Not all things may be forgivable. To find resolution, some say, "My father did the best he could; he didn't know any better." Some reach out to their dads; others do not. There is no right or wrong here; it's what is right for each daughter.

When a young girl loses her "princess-ness" due to her father's actions, and is plunged into the "quagmire," she experiences the shift in a negative, debilitating way. Yet, her very "frog-ness" holds the possibility of rebirth. That is because, though sidetracked, the daughter has within her the potential to develop the tools to get herself unstuck. Like in a fairy tale, she will likely need to develop patience and trust, be willing to seek outside help, and have a sincere desire to heal. The Princess Frog is not doomed; if she can break the spell that keeps her immobilized and at times robbed of her humanness, she will be able to move on in the direction of compassion, courage, and wholeness.

Although the daughter at this stage is able to see her parts, she is actually "undivided" because she has integrated those components into a whole. It is a paradox in that she is made up of many "slices," yet is nevertheless a complete "pie." She may need to continue to dispel the troublesome Judge or face the dark Shadow within, yet she accepts that these pieces are a part of her. To not disown them is to be whole.

Just like the woman at the end of the fairytale who walks towards the "warm, golden sun" hanging over the "round, green meadow," so may The Princess Frog begin to see round shapes of wholeness in her dreams. In her waking life, she might become attracted to round-shaped images, such as the sun, the rainbow, or the butterfly (which also holds the symbol of metamorphosis).

Chapter Two

Stumbling From Princess to Frog

A young girl lives happily with her father. She feels safe, loved, and special. She trusts him completely, but one day his behavior changes. He does something strange, unexplained, hurtful, or out of character that causes her to feel abandoned in some way by him.

This is because, in that moment, he gives up his role as The Good Father. The boundary previously in place to keep the daughter secure and safe is now compromised.

The result of the shift in the relationship creates suffering, confusion, and disruption in the life of the daughter. As she grows older, more than her self-esteem is affected. Her interpersonal relationships, achievements, sexuality, femininity, and ability to trust can all be impacted.

The story of The Princess Frog has at its core the kind of father who basically surrenders his appropriate function with respect to his daughter. He may do so deliberately by "turning away" from her, as in the case of desertion, neglect, betrayal or detachment. He may also turn away indirectly or inadvertently through disinterest, alcoholism, ignorance, helplessness, mistreatment of other family members, illness, or even death. In either case—intentionally or not—the father gives up his proper role, thereby replacing a healthy boundary with a "barrier" within the relationship, serving to keep his daughter cut off from him.

Instead of turning away from his daughter, a dad may inappropriately "turn toward" her through seduction, incest (or the threat of it), emotional or physical abuse … even excessive hovering or "smothering". This type of abandonment tears down the healthy boundary that must exist to keep the daughter both safe and autonomous. The result leaves nothing to prevent the father from blurring the lines between her and him.

These types of actions performed by the father ... turning away from or turning toward the daughter ... can be accomplished either blatantly or subtly. Some are so subtle (as in cases of mild seduction like flirting or veiled emotional putdowns), that she may not trust herself to believe they are happening or are of much importance.

The following page shows a few of the results an abandoning father can produce in his daughter, as seen through her attempts to maneuver within the world of men.

For a woman to begin to deal with the father-wound she endured while growing up, she must be willing to go on the heroine's journey. The metaphor of change from cherished princess to humble frog serves as the starting point on her path to healing and her ultimate opportunity for balance, wholeness, and peace. It is through this process that a woman can begin to reclaim that part of herself that was sacrificed so long ago when her father, for whatever reason, abandoned his sacred role.

ANATOMY OF A "FROG"
SOME CHARACTERISTICS OF THE PRINCESS FROG
IN RELATION TO MEN

INTERNALIZED CHARACTERISTICS	EXTERNALIZED CHARACTERISTICS
Feelings:	**Actions:**
vulnerable	uses sarcasm
shame	sets up barriers: few to no relationships with men
guilt	has strained relationships with men
insecure	has dependent relations with men (no boundaries)
confused	chooses men who will abandon her
mistrustful	abandons men (first)
awkward	seeks men out
shy	shuns men
fear (of abandonment, intimacy)	attempts to be mother or daughter to men
anger and rage	smothers, engulfs men
isolated	withholds from men
aimless	attempts to control men
restless	sacrifices for men
anxious	acts out sexually or is frigid
Needs:	tests men to see if they will leave
validation and reassurance	acts in ways to get attention, approval; flirts
affection	seeks out father figures
attention	lacks responsibility; blames
distance	seeks unattainable men
closeness	acts childish
control	is cruel
Psychological Tendencies:	
projects negative traits onto men	
idealizes men	
cuts off or shuts down emotions or	
parts of herself	

Chapter Three

Saving The Princess Frog

How can The Princess Frog heal herself and move forward?

For The Princess Frog to heal, she needs to become aware of what happened to her.

She must come to understand that the real tragedy for her is not that she is no longer a "princess", for all young princesses must "die" in time. The tragedy is that she was robbed so early, so abruptly. She was not allowed to die a natural death, a necessary death, in order to grow up. Her normal progression towards adulthood was thwarted. Instead of nature taking it's course, her father interfered and snatched away that which she still needed. Just as a young child will in time give up a bottle, a pacifier, a favorite blanket, etc., she would have given up her princess needs and moved on to other, more mature roles. The difference is, if things had occurred in a natural way, her esteem and a sense of power would have likely remained intact. It is because the process was prematurely and brutally interrupted, the wounding occurred.

Had the princess been allowed to stay in the "castle" during her formative years, she ultimately would have come to leave, both of her own accord and with the help of her wise father-king. Though no longer a princess, she would have carried her princess-ness within, to reflect on fondly, to draw strength from, to build on.

She must also realize that what happened to her was not her fault. It was not that she wasn't good enough or that she did something wrong. The reality is that the responsibility rested with her father, who neglected or poorly handled his role. (Loving fathers, who unwillfully abandoned their daughters by dying, by being denied access to them, or by struggling with incapacitating illness, are not accountable.)

For The Princess Frog to heal, she needs to mourn what has been lost to her.

The sadness and rage associated with the realization of what she has suffered and been denied, must be acknowledged, must be felt. She needs to be willing to go through the pain of mourning. This can be encouraged through therapy; it can occur in everyday living. Or both.

Psychiatrist Elisabeth Kübler-Ross in her book, "On Death and Dying," famously identified five stages of grief: denial, anger, bargaining, depression, and acceptance. Not everyone follows these stages in the order set, and individuals can skip stages, repeat stages, or be in more than one at a time. However, The Princess Frog can expect to go through some form of these stages when in mourning. In the fairytale, the frog awakens dazed and in denial. She experiences anger ... even rage ... in relation to the little lost ant. She falls into a depression when she tumbles into the dark cave and has to face her demons. Finally, she finds her way to a place of healing and peace.

For The Princess Frog to heal, she needs to have hope.

She must be willing to take a risk ... to put faith in herself and her ability to heal and grow. She must become her own warrior.

For The Princess Frog to heal, she needs to have some understanding of what healing <u>is.</u>

Healing is a process. It is something that advances towards an end result. It involves transformation.

Traditionally, healing has to do with mending, curing, and restoring. It is related to the concept of wholeness … making something whole (again).

For The Princess Frog to heal, she needs to have some understanding of what healing <u>is</u> <u>not.</u>

We are all different and heal in our own way. However, it is important to remember that healing does not mean the same thing as erasing history. It does not mean that something never happened. We all have scars on our bodies in places where we once suffered wounds: scrapes, sores, infections, bites, surgeries, etc. Though we may no longer bleed from these places or feel the pain once associated with them, they nevertheless remain visible reminders that something unpleasant happened to us. We may feel a bit vulnerable or sensitive in these areas. We may find ourselves more aware of these places on our bodies, maybe try to protect them or cover them up with makeup or clothing if we think they are unsightly. We may even forget about them, unless we are reminded.

Although a tremendous amount of healing can occur, there will always be traces left of the wounding that took place. To be whole is to accept that fact. A gift from one's wounding is the potential for greater sensitivity and compassion toward oneself and others.

For The Princess Frog to heal, she may find herself involved in a natural healing process.

Human beings can grow and heal in spite of obstacles. In spite of having been wounded. In spite of themselves, and without even trying. They mature. They grow up. They get a different perspective. This in no way is meant to discount their pain, but they often see things differently, literally, as they get taller.

A Princess Frog may get involved with or marry a man who possesses Good Father traits. Part of her wound can be healed as he holds her when she gets hurt or feels upset.

He may pamper her and treat her like a princess He may compliment her and truly listen to what she has to say.

She may get some healing by watching how men struggle in their role as fathers, realizing it's not so easy for them to always be the Good King to their daughters. She may come to understand fathers are human, wrestling with life's challenges, and often quite wounded themselves.

As she gains perspective, The Princess Frog can find it healing to know that what a father says and does might have a great deal to do with the generation or culture from which he comes. For example, that those things she may have missed, such as compliments, may not have come from a place of insensitivity or uncaring, but rather from the sincere belief and desire on his part not to spoil his child.

For The Princess Frog to heal, she may need to first find, and then be willing to receive, help.

She needs resources in order to heal. But she must be careful. Because she has a blind spot when it comes to men, she must choose others who will help to heal her rather than feed into and perpetuate her wounded process. Aside from seeking healthy relationships, one of the first and wisest things she can do is look for a good mental health professional. It is the conscious commitment to deal with the unconscious via the therapeutic process that often holds the greatest potential for her growth and healing. This is because therapy holds the opportunity for gaining true insight and tools, which will continue to serve and enlighten her through the losses and abandonments yet to come.

It would be helpful if the therapist specializes in issues of abandonment in the father-daughter relationship. A competent therapist will need to carry both the roles of the Good Mother (providing nurturing, compassion, understanding, and caring) and the Good Father (encouraging risk, championing growth, challenging inappropriate behaviors, and setting and honoring appropriate boundaries).

Those healthy boundaries in the therapeutic relationship are maintained by the therapist and have to do with consistency and safety, such as: scheduled appointments that adhere to set time frames, a consistent physical environment, confidentiality, and a strict moral code (including no seductive behavior or crossing sexual barriers).

In the therapeutic relationship, The Princess Frog will discover what it is like to be in a healthy relationship with another person, will become aware of what has happened to her, how she acts and feels as a result, and begin to build her own internal resources.

Often the best way to find a therapist is by referral from a friend or professional, like her doctor. She may be impressed hearing one speak at a conference and pursue that avenue. In any event, it is a good idea to ask for a consultation and interview one or more therapists to see how she feels in his or her presence. Does she feel understood? Does she feel respected? Cared about? Safe? Comfortable? Are there boundaries? Ask the therapist about his/her philosophy, how s/he works, and his/ her experience with women who have been abandoned in some way by their fathers.

And, of course, a healthy relationship is not only potentially found in a therapist's office. To be in a healthy relationship means to be involved with someone who is at peace with himself/herself and is willing to empower others and encourage them to find their own sense of fulfillment. Being in the presence of such a person will be very apparent to The Princess Frog because she will feel enhanced and elevated by the encounter. She will feel better about herself and carry away a sense of hope. To be in a healthy relationship with someone, whether therapist, spouse, lover, friend, etc., is to be in a meaningful one.

One resource The Princess Frog has always had and probably never knew about or encouraged, would be her dreams. With help from her therapist, she can begin to explore what her dreams are attempting to communicate to her and how they can help her to heal.

Over time, due to the therapeutic process, the daughter will develop the ability to be more conscious. She will be able to analyze interactions with others, be aware of her feelings: with whom she feels joyous or tortured, honored or discounted, equal or unequal.

As mentioned earlier, she can also develop greater consciousness through awareness of her parts and learn to organize them in ways that serve her, rather than fragment and weaken her.

The Princess Frog will need help on the outside. She will need to be in a healthy relationship with someone who can guide her, someone with first-hand understanding of the healing process, a person who has been there and come out on the other side. This can be a wise mentor, a friend, or a good therapist.

Getting help is like going back, securing the weak foundation of a house, and rebuilding from there. Can The Princess Frog be helped? Yes!

For The Princess Frog to fully heal, she may need to make meaning out of the wounding.

Eventually, in the process of healing, she has the opportunity to go beyond merely healing the wound, and perhaps forgiving her father. She has the possibility of developing the potential to be who she really is and find her own worth, her own set of values, world view, and true nature.

To do so, she will need to see her wounding as a symbol and, with love and wisdom, come to embrace it. The changing of a princess into a frog can <u>ultimately</u> be a step up ... not a step down.

This is a profoundly personal process, one in which each individual must come to herself. Wounding might be seen as a religious symbol: one's cross to bear. Or, it might represent an important life lesson, a badge of courage, a symbol of survival and strength, or a vehicle that enabled The Princess Frog to become a more loving, compassionate human being,

Seeking wholeness, resolution, and peace, The Princess Frog must be willing to risk entering the realm of the unknown ... uncharted territory ... calling upon others and parts of herself to guide, teach and heal her. She must honor the wounded "frog" within her. She must reclaim her own sense of the specialness she felt long ago.

If it sounds like magic, in a sense it is. This is, indeed, a magical, mysterious journey. Some would call it a spiritual one. It is a venture upon which courageous souls dare to set forth. Will you?

Chapter Four

Seeking The Good Father

Pediatrician and psychoanalyst, Donald Winnicott (1896-1971), maintained that the healthy emotional development of a child is not dependent on a perfect mother, but rather, on a "good enough mother." He refers to the "ordinary devoted mother" who responds to her baby's needs and over time encourages his or her independence.

Similarly, a dad, though imperfect, can strive to be The Good Father … that is, a good enough father. Because of the nature of many families today, mother and father roles often are interchangeable. Still, there resides in our human collective psyche, as well as in our heritage of traditional roles, a sense of what a Good Father is.

In the father-daughter relationship, a healthy dad helps to relax the often overly enmeshed bond between the daughter and her mother that can ultimately keep the daughter dependent. He introduces his daughter to the greater world … beyond the mother … and shows her how to maneuver within it. His goal is to prepare her for an independent, responsible life: to be able to eventually leave the family free of guilt, prepared to face life's challenges. While moms often cling, a Good Father encourages problem solving and discovering new things. He invites her to risk. To dare. He is likely the one to teach his daughter how to ride a bike, write a check, or catch a fish.

The Good Father attempts to stand firm in his role no matter what. He remains consistently available to, accepting of, and communicative with his daughter. He makes time for her. He is sensitive to her needs and respects them. He understands his role as confidant, mediator, protector, and teacher. He accepts the commitment and responsibility that raising a child entails.

The competent dad attends to his daughter's femininity in a non-seductive manner; he gives her the impression that it is something to be cherished and valued. He pays her compliments; he tells her she is beautiful, and he means it.

Because he plays a significant role in the emotional development of his daughter, he does not abuse his own power, but rather is cognizant of his part in developing a sense of power in his daughter. He builds her confidence and esteem by applauding both her efforts and her successes.

When his child is young, a Good Father will often become his daughter's first playmate. He loves to make her laugh, carry her around on his shoulders, act silly.

Being the first male in her life, he knows he represents what a man, husband, and father should be. He wants to be her hero.

He defends her when appropriate. Ever the teacher, he lends his support and shares his perspectives. He is there to comfort and advise her when she makes mistakes or feels stuck in a problem. Though his love is apt to be somewhat conditional, in that he will expect her to follow the rules and take the consequences for her mistakes, only what she does will be judged, not who she is.

A Good Father misses the mark now and then. He drops the ball at times. He can get cranky, tired, self-absorbed … like any human being. But because he has good intent, and because he is devoted to the relationship, it does not take long before he turns his attention to what needs to be done to get back on track. He apologizes. If he feels awkward or decides he has been somewhat insensitive, he shares those thoughts with his daughter. He is accountable to her because the relationship is to be cherished, preserved, nurtured, and constantly redefined if it is to continue to fulfill it's task.

Even though periodically off track, a caring father never crosses a certain boundary with his daughter. It is a boundary that both protects her and their relationship at all costs. A strong boundary is built into the structure of all emotionally healthy families. The Good Father is aware of, respects, and therefore adheres to what might be called:

THE HEALTHY FAMILY HIERARCHY

MOM AND DAD, a team, are at the top ... co-parenters and leaders in charge.

....

A BOUNDARY keeps the "line" between parents and children from blurring.

....

THE CHILDREN are staggered according to age; as children grow up, both their privileges and responsibilities increase.

The boundary within the hierarchal family is a limit, a "stop sign," a line of separation. Emotionally healthy parents do not cross this line nor do they allow their children to do so. The boundary serves as a loving safety net to all parties. It keeps people from getting "lost" in each other, and provides individuals the freedom to be themselves and grow.

When a father tampers with the boundary in relation to his daughter, he abandons her. He also abandons himself, in that he abandons his Good Father role. Boundaries are complex because they serve to both "hold in" and "keep out." That is, they hold in each person's separateness as well as the relationship itself, while keeping out the threat of merger or danger.

The Good Father understands the importance of the roles played in the family, so he is able to handle whatever his daughter may do. He understands that girls become infatuated with their fathers, attempt to practice on them, or test the rules, often when new feelings emerge. He realizes that he, too, might experience new emotions, but that he needn't feel threatened by them or feel tempted to act on them inappropriately. He reminds himself of his role.

Children are allowed to test the rules and may act out in order to discover what is safe and what is acceptable behavior. They must be able to do so in a contained environment ... one that is boundaried. Should the father's position in the hierarchy be challenged by the daughter, he gently lets her know that her place in the family is to be a kid, not an adult. Though all are permitted a voice in the family, it is not a democracy; parents are in charge.

When it comes to the hierarchy, good dads respect both children and those with whom they co-parent. It has been said that the greatest gift a father can give his children is to treat their mother with respect. I might add: whether he is still married to her or not. He never uses his daughter as a pawn, or tries to turn her against her mother.

The Good Father doesn't give up his responsibilities by looking to his growing daughter for nurturing, or use her as a sounding board for his personal problems or worries. He doesn't make her his friend, lover, "parent," or emotional/physical punching bag. Nor does he turn his back on her.

The healthy family hierarchy allows for daughters to have a childhood unburdened by the inappropriateness of their fathers. When dads hold to their healthy role, they remain safe and approachable. In this way, daughters need never be wounded. Loving intent and boundaries are key.

Though no father is perfect, he can learn, often with the help of therapy, consciousness, and goodwill, to appreciate and live out the role of The Good Father. Dads need to become aware of the importance of their participation in the formation of their daughters' lives and how the abandoning of their role serves to wound the very souls who so depend on them and who so love them.

Author's Note

- As a therapist, I stand on the shoulders of those who precede me in the field of psychology—the creators of theories who have come to define what we psychotherapists do in our profession. Throughout the years, I have garnered ideas, models, strategies, techniques, procedures, and skills … not always aware or sure of the source. I am indebted to those innovators for their contributions and have endeavored to give them credit whenever possible.

- In the early 1980s, I read a scholarly book that brought the issue of abandoning fathers to my attention: *The Wounded Woman: Healing the Father-Daughter Relationship,* by Linda Schierse Leonard. Her account sensitized me to the problem and enabled me to see for myself the effect father-wounding had on many of my female clients. As a result, some of Leonard's findings … those which I personally discovered/experienced in my work as a therapist … are incorporated into my creation of The Princess Frog.

- The range and teachings of Swiss psychiatrist and psychotherapist, Carl Jung, hold a respected place in my professional background as a therapist. His theory of Analytical Psychology has been prominent in the way I've practiced, and, unless otherwise indicated, his ideas in some form live on most of the pages in this book. The text reflects my interpretation as well ... my ideas, input, and original stamp. The fairy tale, a narrative based on the healing process, is my creation alone. I have purposely eliminated some of Jung's technical terms and chosen instead to keep his concepts more easily understandable. I hope I have succeeded in that endeavor. A Jungian therapist once told me there are two kinds of Jungians: those of the head and those of the heart. I am of the heart, and it is in that spirit I have approached the subject of healing in the father-daughter relationship.

Appendices

Appendix A

THE SHADOW

IMPORTANT: Please do not go on to the next page until completing this exercise, in order to insure a valuable result.

Answer the following 8 questions using only a few words or short phrases:

1. How do you see yourself?

2. How do you think others see you?

3. How would you like others to see you?

4. How realistic or possible is it for others to see you this way? (refers to #3)

5. Describe the personality you find most despicable or impossible to get along with.

6. What makes you angry about others?

7. What traits do you most envy in others?

8. Describe an impression you've given to someone and didn't mean to. (This could have happened once or many times.)

When you have completed this exercise, you may go on to the next page for an explanation.

EXPLANATION OF EXERCISE

I discovered this exercise while a graduate student in a PhD program in Psychology at California Graduate Institute in Westwood, California, during the 1980s.

You have completed an exercise based on the work of Carl Jung, founder of Analytical Psychology. According to Jung, the exercise you did in Appendix A would be broken down this way:

Questions 1-4:

These questions deal with what Jung called the "PERSONA", or the mask we wear in the world. It is largely conscious, and it is the way we tend to identify ourselves: the part of us concerned with how we look to ourselves and others, our status in the community.

Questions 5-8:

These questions have to do with what Jung called the "SHADOW", or the unconscious part of ourselves that lies in darkness. Why? Because we either don't like those traits (as in the case of #s 5, 6, and 8: the Negative Shadow), or we don't even realize we have the potential for, or already possess, the very traits we envy in others (as in the case of # 7: the Positive Shadow).

So, reread your answers to #s 5-8 with the understanding that you have accessed your Shadow piece and have been describing yourself!

What? You object? That can't be you? Think again. Every person answers differently because every person has his or her own unique Shadow. We're all human and have the capacity for possessing the same human traits, but some are specific to us when it comes to our dark side.

Why is this important, and what does this have to do with the subject of this book? On the road to healing and growing, it is important to know and accept all our parts. It is one of the ways to heal and become the whole person we can be. Knowledge is power and the more we understand how we tick and why, the better we can cope and protect ourselves as we live our lives.

Let's say you are attending a lecture and someone stands up in the audience and makes a comment. If you experience a very strong negative reaction to that person (the content of what s/he says, the tone or inflection of the voice, body language, physical looks, etc.), there is a good chance your Shadow is involved.

When you have a strong reaction to someone, you can ask yourself two questions.

The first is:

HOW AM I LIKE THIS PERSON?

Perhaps it seems to you that those who stand up and speak in front of a large group of people must be pretty full of themselves. Ask yourself if you ever have snobby thoughts and feelings, or if you boast and brag at times. Maybe these thoughts, feelings or comments surprise or disappoint you when they occur. Or, perhaps, more importantly, you are unaware of this bragging part of yourself. By asking how you are like this person, you can access your Negative Shadow and bring it "home" to you, instead of seeing it "out there" in others.

If you ask yourself question #1 but honestly don't believe you are like that person, then ask yourself the second question: HOW MIGHT I ENVY THIS PERSON?

This is the Positive Shadow. Maybe what really bothers you is that this person is able to speak in front of others with great ease ... something you wish you could do. Or look that attractive. Or sound so intelligent. Sometimes we don't acknowledge our strong points or weren't complimented growing up, so we lack self esteem. Think of the beautiful girl who thinks she's ugly ... I've known many in my practice.

The reality may be that you are the very thing you wish you were. You just don't know it. By asking yourself how you might envy someone, you bring what you envy to you, instead of seeing it only "out there." Once you realize that you may already be the person you wish you were, or that you could do something to develop that characteristic (take a speech class; join Toastmasters, etc.), you are in a position to grow.

When you ask yourself these 2 questions, you stop projecting onto others and begin to work on you. By knowing your weaknesses and strengths, you have the awareness necessary to make positive changes in your life. By accepting ALL your parts, you can decide how to conduct yourself ... what kind of person you truly want to be.

It is not enough to get through the pain of an old wound. The opportunity is there for you to become a whole person. What is a whole person? One who is in balance and at peace.

Appendix B

DREAMS

Dreams are known to emerge from the realm of the unconscious, often in ways which leave the dreamer confused, amused, elated, or terrorized. Instead of presenting themselves in a nicely organized fashion, dreams often offer up bizarre scenarios and features making it difficult for us to decipher.

A variety of books are available to help the daughter begin to explore the meanings of the symbolic language found in dreams. There are many approaches one may take ... too many to discuss here.

But let's take a look at one of the dreams the frog had in the fairytale: the one in which she was being chased by teeth-gnashing dogs. The following are some ideas The Princess Frog might use in working with this dream:

First, she could ask herself, "How did I feel in the dream?"

If she felt scared, she could then think about what is scary in her life. Perhaps it's fear of getting ripped apart, maybe through a relationship (like what happened with Dad); it could be fear of annihilation, such as not being able to survive emotional pain; or possibly a fear of being devoured, as in being eaten alive with constant memories of the past, which is ever on her heels.

If she felt hunted in the dream, the daughter could ask herself how she's being "stalked" in her current life, perhaps by invasive memories of her father-loss. Is something "chasing" her or closing in on her? This approach helps The Princess

Frog to get in touch with her feelings and affords her the opportunity to take some sort of action, such as talk about it to a close confidant or enter therapy. There will be more ideas for taking action in the various appendices to follow.

It has been said that one may approach dreams as if the dreamer is every part of the dream: in this case, the running frog, the dogs, their teeth, the actual road the frog and dogs are running on, etc. The Princess Frog might question in what way she is like the snarling dogs, the flashing teeth, etc. What is she running after: the fantasy of how it could have been with her father? What is she chewing on: the abandonment or rejection? How she hates men? Etc.

Another way for the daughter to work with a dream involves choosing an element from it on which to focus. For example, she could run to the nearest dream symbol book and look up "dog." There she will find ideas as to what a dog represents. These are known as Universal Symbols … what most people think of when thinking of dogs or what cultures have universally adopted as their attributes.

First, however, I would encourage her to ask herself what comes to mind when thinking of dogs. This will help her to identify her own Personal Symbols. A universal symbol may portray "dog" in ways that are different from the association the dreamer has with it. The personal experiences and feelings we bring to dream elements often give us a more accurate analysis of our dreams. For example, in a symbol book, the dog might be identified as a guardian of the soul (perhaps in the dream as a call to consciousness). But let's say the dreamer had been bitten in the past; to the dreamer, the dog might be identified as a merciless killer, intent on destroying that very soul. After understanding her own symbol, she can then examine the universal one. How different "dog" will be seen from these two perspectives when analyzing the dream. Both may be useful to the dreamer.

Another technique in dream work can involve dialoguing, perhaps on a piece of paper, with an element in the dream:

Dreamer:	"What are you doing in my dream?"
Dog:	"I'm going to kill you."
Dreamer:	"Why would you do that?"
Dog:	"Because you're weak (scared, easy prey, unimportant, etc.)."

This discussion can end in a variety of ways, which can prove enlightening to the dreamer.

For an interesting, more in-depth experience with dream work, I recommend, *Inner Work: Using Dreams and Active Imagination for Personal Growth* by Robert A. Johnson.

No matter how or how much a dream is analyzed, it is important to remember that, by it's very nature, there usually remains a little mystery to it.

Appendix C

THE JUDGE (or Inner Critic)

Somewhere along the line, The Princess Frog must deal with The Judge: the part of her that makes her feel bad about herself. This occurs because she is breaking an unspoken rule:

"Thou shalt not feel good about thyself."

The inner critic reinforces the message the daughter received as a result of her father's betrayal and abandonment … as if it is reminding her, "Of course your father abandoned you; you are worthless."

The Princess Frog may also feel unrecognizable to herself. She may feel threatened and awkward in her new skin, which may tempt her to return to her old familiar self, no matter how dysfunctional.

It is important that she keep the critical part of herself in check. A good way to begin is to get to know her Judge by doing the following exercise.

EXERCISE: FINDING YOUR JUDGE

Have crayons, colored pens or pencils and a sheet of paper at hand.

A. Sit in a quiet place and close your eyes. Allow an image of your Judge to come to mind.

If you, YOURSELF, appear as The Judge, try again. We're talking about a PART or PIECE of you ... not all of you ... even if it feels that way.

Your Judge:
- may be masculine, feminine, or neutral.
- could be a complete figure of a body, or part of a body.
- might be an object.
- may only be a color.
- could be abstract ... something unique.
- might resemble a courtroom judge.
- may be a feeling, which can be expressed through color.

B. When you have something in mind, open your eyes and select a crayon or crayons (etc.) to represent the image. (Note: your Judge is present if you feel intimidated, awkward, or are telling yourself, "I can't draw ... " Forge on, and remember you do not have to share this picture with anyone else.)

Now draw your Judge, remembering it will not look exactly like the image in your mind. To do so is neither possible, nor necessary. And this has nothing to do with talent; you have accessed your unconscious mind, which is the purpose of the exercise. You don't have to make an elaborate drawing ... just a quick, simple one works fine.

When you are finished, you will have something to always remember: what your very own Judge looks like.

C. Study your drawing.

How do you feel looking at it? Is there anything about it that resembles or reminds you of someone in your life ... currently or in the past? If so, that could be useful information in understanding where your Judge comes from. It may be a manifestation of the critical parent you encountered growing up who always told you that you were doing something wrong, or led you to believe you were no good.

This critical part of us can also speak for society or religious doctrine, creating feelings such as shame, guilt, and fear in a person who is struggling to find her own truth or her own path.

Note the color or colors you chose to signify your Judge. Why do you think you selected those particular ones? What do they mean to you? Many people opt for black, gray or dark colors; others pick hues they dislike. Some choose colors that suggest the feelings they associate with their Judge. Others don't know why they have chosen the colors they did. Perhaps it will come to them at a later time.

D. Now that you have drawn your Judge, you can take some ACTION, which gives you a sense of power and keeps you from getting "caught" in bad feelings.

YOU CAN DO SOMETHING PHYSICAL with the picture itself, such as:
1. Rip it up, throw it away, bury it, or burn it.
2. You may trap it in an envelope or a container.

YOU CAN USE YOUR IMAGINATION.

1. Knowing what your Judge looks like, imagine it shrinking down to the size of an ant ... then squish it with your thumb.

2. Put your inner critic in a plastic column and watch its words get trapped inside, unable to reach you.

YOU CAN USE YOUR VOICE (outloud or in your head).

1. Banish your Judge from the room, your town, the universe, etc.

2. When you find yourself feeling attacked by the put-downs in your head, say: "deflect" and imagine those negative words falling away from you.

3. Tell your critical piece that it is lying and that you refuse to listen to those lies. There may be a kernel of truth in what it says, but basically The Judge does whatever it takes to sabotage you and keep you down. A daughter with low self-esteem will believe whatever supports the idea that she is worthless ... even if it means listening to lies. Don't fall into that trap; you are better than that!

You may be asking yourself why it is so important to know what The Judge looks like and whether it's really that necessary to talk to it and take action against it. The point is to make it as real as possible, because that destructive piece that lives in all of us to some degree is real. Unlike our conscience, which serves to direct us in positive, ethical ways, our critic holds us back and robs us of living a full, productive, joyous life. With the conscience, there is heart; with The Judge there is none.

Working with this destructive piece begins by recognizing when it is present. As soon as you do, take some sort of action as suggested above, or create your own way of dealing with it. If you don't realize what is happening at first, that's okay ... take action when you do, even hours or days later. In time, you'll note it rather quickly. Remember that awareness is the first step in this process.

The more you incorporate these actions, the more positive results you will experience. The Judge never fully goes away; it will always pop up again. However, in time it will appear less often and its effect will be greatly weakened. It's not the fact that it surfaces; how you handle it when it does, is what's important.

A great by-product of working with the inner critic is that you will come to recognize those who support and encourage you, and those, like The Judge, who drag you down. When you banish the destructiveness of The Judge, you may begin to challenge or weed out toxic people in your life. Then, internally and in the world, you are truly standing up for yourself. That is a sign of good self-esteem.

Appendix D

THE INNER CHILD

The daughter, in the course of healing, may begin to pay more attention to the wounded princess part of herself. This can occur by her developing greater compassion toward those in pain, or through her receiving tender care and concern from others. For some daughters, this awareness can take a long time.

Because she was abandoned as a child, she often adds to her trauma by spurning and despising that part of her which still resides within: what popular psychology calls her Inner Child. (It is believed to have originated from Jung's concept of The Divine Child.) Repulsed, it is not uncommon for The Princess Frog to do to herself what others she most cared for, did to her. That which was modeled, is powerful. Betrayed, rejected, even ignored through father-wounding, she perpetuates her grief through self-sabotage, self-loathing, impatience, and repulsion. No matter how wonderful she may treat children or how sensitive she might be toward the needs of The Inner Child of others, The Princess Frog often disclaims, denigrates and turns a cold shoulder to that part of herself which so desires her love, comfort and acceptance. The wounded Inner Child waits and waits, sometimes a lifetime, to be seen ... to be found.

Through the giving and receiving of compassion, the daughter can begin to entertain the notion that perhaps she has value. She may not be more important than anyone else, but neither is she less significant. If compassion is a human emotion, maybe she could learn to find some for herself.

When a daughter suffers a father-wound, the time at which the trauma takes place remains frozen in her psyche. Subsequently, when things happen to her reminiscent of the shift in the relationship with her father (feeling abandoned, rejected, betrayed, ignored, etc.), she will often respond as that internal child. For example, if the shift came at age 10, the daughter will likely have a 10-year-old Inner Child who could express her fear, sadness, anxiety and anger in the way an actual 10-year-old does. If fearful, she may want to hide or run to someone she feels safe with; she could say she's "scared" (a child's word) instead of "frightened" (an adult's word). When sad, she might whine or sob. With anxiety, she may become needy, clingy, and feel very small and vulnerable. Angry, she could throw a tantrum and scream. These are all clues that the "child" in her, instead of her grownup part, is reacting and in charge.

With this awareness, the daughter has the opportunity to work with the Unfinished Business connected to her Inner Child. By honoring the "separate" wounded portion of herself, she can ultimately incorporate it into her total being.

But how can this transformation take place? The Princess Frog, through father-wounding, lacks self-esteem. Though she may gather some initially through her career, through therapy, a close, loving relationship, etc., there is no compensating for her loss and pain like the care she can learn to give to herself. For, who better knows what she needs? Who is always there? As The Princess Frog learns to focus on her feelings when engaged with others, she is attending to her Inner Child and protecting her from psychological harm: Do I feel safe right now with this person? Am I starting to doubt myself? Not feel good about me? Does my radar tell me not to reveal too much of myself? Do I feel like getting away from him or her? Do I really want to do this, or am I only trying to please this person at my expense?

Good self-care leads to self-esteem. Learning to comfort and protect her internal child, The Princess Frog can grow and heal. The more real she makes her Inner Child, the more confident, peaceful and whole the daughter can become as a person ... and the greater the opportunity for The Wise Woman to ultimately emerge. But this process does take time; this material needs to be read and digested several times, as well as practiced faithfully, until healing occurs and good self-care becomes automatic.

The three exercises on the following pages are designed for The Princess Frog to begin a relationship with her internal child.

EXERCISE #1: ASKING YOURSELF THESE QUESTIONS

Can I see that my current hurt, angry, sad, or fearful feelings and responses may be connected to the part of me that was wounded through the relationship I had with my father?

Could this be how I felt as a child at the time of the shift? Or at some point thereafter?

When I think back on when the wounding took place, how old was I? (If you can't remember, then come up with a number or a range that sounds right to you: an infant? sometime during the first 5 years? elementary school years? adolescence?)

Will I make the effort to honor my Inner Child by locating a photo of me at that age … a photo that I will put in a special frame, in a place where I can view it daily to see how small, dear, and innocent she is? If I'm unable to see these qualities, can I imagine her being someone else's child … one I can value? In other words, would I treat that child the way I treat myself? (The point of this exercise is to begin to develop a connection between the little girl you were when you got hurt, and the wounded internal child who consequently still lives on inside of you.)

If I still have trouble caring about my Inner Child, can I perhaps achieve that compassion for her through the love and tenderness I feel toward my pet? (Like pets, children are defenseless and at the mercy of the situation in which they find themselves. Both are dependent upon others for safety and security, can be mistreated, experience loss, and grieve.

Therefore, if you can come to associate the wounded part of yourself with the vulnerability of a beloved animal, you might be able to use your pet love as a springboard to Inner Child love.)

When I see children of the age I was when the shift with my father occurred, will I take the time to stop and get a sense of their innocence and need for protection and attention?

Can I imagine my reaching out to my Inner Child when I feel scared or alone? Trying to comfort that part of myself as if she were a real child? Envisioning picking her up, hugging her, placing her in my lap, or putting her behind me to shield her from harm? Allowing her to express her feelings? (She's been longing for you to find her and take care of her. How long will you keep her waiting, now that you know she exists? No one can take better care of her than you because you, more than anyone else, know what she needs.)

Can I take a leap of faith and trust that Inner Child Work is a wonderful tool in healing The Princess Frog?

EXERCISE #2: DIALOGUING ON PAPER WITH YOUR INNER CHILD

Princess Frog: "What's wrong?"
Inner Child: "I feel angry."
PF: "Why?"
IC: "You're so busy."
PF: "Well, I have to work."
IC: "But there's no time for me."
PF: "So, what is it you want to do?"
IC: "I want to go to the movies (bake cookies, listen to music, etc.)."
PF: "Okay, tomorrow between 3:00 and 5:00, we'll play."

You may be amazed at what can come out in a dialogue, as in this example. You have the opportunity to get to know more about your Inner Child and what she needs in order to heal.

Remember that the internal child part of you may wonder if you will really follow through on your promises, so be sure that you do. If not, you will re-wound her and likely undo any progress you've made. Also, it's important that promises are realistic and can be fulfilled.

The Inner Child needs strong boundaries; she may go to anger if she can't get her needs met immediately. However, if you consistently keep your word, she will learn that she'll get the time and attention she's been promised. She will come to trust you.

When the grown daughter makes a place for her internal child, that child can get healing. And the relationship itself can bring balance and wholeness to The Princess Frog.

EXERCISE #3: CHANGING THE TRAUMATIC INCIDENTS OF THE PAST

Healing one's Inner Child can also occur by "going back" to those life incidents in which she was wounded, and "changing" them. For example, if the young daughter was molested by a family member, she could return to the memory in her imagination, with one important difference. Where, in the past, she was a defenseless child alone in a room with the perpetrator, she now has an ally present: her grownup self. In the fantasy, the adult she is today is there to protect the child she was then, in any way she can.

It could be done VERBALLY:

For example: the adult could say, "Don't you dare touch that child! " "Stop! I won't allow you to mistreat her." "Take your hands off of her ... what you are doing is evil, and I will do whatever it takes to keep that from happening."

It could be done PHYSICALLY:

For example: the adult could place herself between the child and the perpetrator, or remove the child altogether from the situation. Or, the adult could physically wrestle with or beat up the perpetrator. (In other words, the adult allows herself to do WHATEVER IT TAKES to be victorious in saving the child.)

Of course, this technique can be used not only in cases of molestation, but certainly in all father-wounding incidents, such as physical or emotional abuse, betrayal, abandonment, etc.

There are several advantages to this technique, including the fact that no one in reality is actually getting hurt (see Appendix G: the Fantasy section in Confronting the Father)

The adult daughter is building a trusting relationship with her Inner Child.

The actual incident can seem somehow strangely altered by this fantasy; envisioning it differently somehow helps to make it different.

The alteration gives the adult daughter the opportunity to experience an important feeling of power and a sense of justice.

Another by-product of this exercise is that it can serve as a dress rehearsal for life. Once a daughter experiences standing up for her Inner Child in fantasy, she often is able to do so in reality. Suddenly she can find the voice to stick up for herself. Unexpectedly she may see that her Inner Child is suffering in a relationship, and it is no longer acceptable to be silent about it or remain stuck in it.

Appendix E

TRANCE STATES

There are several ways to begin to heal the wounded internal child (See Appendix D: The Inner Child). What can get in the way of success, however, occurs when The Princess Frog falls into a particular trance ... one in which she loses her humanity, her compassion, and her heart.

We humans fall into trances all the time. We all have driven somewhere, deep in thought, and can't remember how we got there. Some know what it feels like to get swept up in a religious or political discussion only to later regret having said certain things. Music, books, films, lectures, falling in love ... all can get a hold on us and transport us.

Trance states may also "kick in" as we carry out our various roles, such as the mom who jumps into a freezing river to save her drowning child; a peace-loving soldier, who would never kill under normal circumstances, now shoots without hesitation at the enemy; an average group of people can become incited and turn into a mob.

We gently slip into a trance state or jump into it like a light switch suddenly turned on. It's as if we are seized and held captive. It can run its course for seconds, minutes, months, even years. We're usually unaware we are in one at the time; that's when we might afterwards hear ourselves say, "I don't know what got into me; that's not me."

Some trance states are enjoyable, life-enhancing, or desirable. Others are not. In the case of The Princess Frog who despises her Inner Child, she may remain firmly stuck. The internal critic (See Appendix C: The Judge) colludes with the wounded daughter's repulsion of her Inner Child and helps keep the trance alive. It's very important for The Frog Princess to break away from that state so she can move on with her life as a whole person, otherwise she will be dragging the anchor of despair up a very steep mountain.

With trance states difficult to break, what can be done? Hope comes with awareness and the desire for change. Begin by identifying what is happening to you. At first it will likely be after the trance occurred … when you look back on it. In time, you might be able to identify it as it is actually happening. But don't be surprised if you remain stuck for a while, even as you observe it taking place. That's how powerful a trance can be. Remember it controls you; you don't control it. The good news is, if you do the work by embracing your Inner Child, this particular trance state can be greatly reduced.

A technique for coming out of this sort of quasi-dream state is to stand up if you are seated, and sit down if you are standing. A shift in the body can sometimes help you to "wake up," or "break the spell," as noted in the fairytale.

Appendix F

USING MASCULINE AND FEMININE ENERGY EFFECTIVELY

Although there are different points of view as to what constitutes masculine and feminine energy, I find it useful to look at some basic ideas. First of all, we are not talking about men being masculine and women being feminine. Rather, we are looking at the notion that all humans, to varying degrees, carry both masculine and feminine qualities. I offer the following discussion in the hope of helping The Princess Frog to understand another aspect of herself that can help her to maneuver in the world more effectively.

When the daughter finds a way of uniting her feminine and masculine energy, her experience of the world changes dramatically. I suggest the feminine brings heart and humanity; the masculine brings head and practicality. Concern for relationship (the feminine) is balanced with good self-care (the masculine). For example, I wanted to impart knowledge to women in need and present it in such a way that it was understandable and useful; this desire is rooted in my feminine-relational part. But it's the masculine-"take charge" portion of me that actually got it written down and published.

Father-wounding can throw off the potential natural balance of the daughter. Suddenly tossed into a sea of drowning confusion, she desperately struggles to stay afloat in any way she can to survive. Some tilt more to the feminine side in their behavior, others to the masculine. Both are coping mechanisms, which attempt to deal with an upside-down world. The problem is hanging on to one or the other, or bouncing between the two, ultimately doesn't work. Only a balance of the two energies working in tandem, promotes healthy behavior.

In order to illustrate this more fully, it helps to know how a person behaves when:

- functioning predominantly from one's feminine part, without benefit of the masculine.
- operating largely from one's masculine side, without the inclusion of the feminine.
- acting from both one's masculine and feminine aspects, as a team.

The meek, often undemonstrative, wounded Princess Frog on one extreme of the spectrum, exhibits traits of the feminine gone amok. She is a dishrag. She values others more than she values herself. She has no power or esteem. Without the strength and drive of the masculine, she is "half" a person.

The bulldozing, overbearing, wounded Princess Frog on the opposite pole, reveals traits of a skewed masculinity. She is a bully. She values herself at the expense of others. She misuses and abuses her power. Without the approachability and thoughtfulness of the feminine, she is "half" a person.

With healing, the daughter, demonstrating traits of both the masculine and feminine in balance, finds her humanity. Her masculine energy helps her stick up for herself and move forward in her life; her feminine energy takes relationship into account by treating herself and others with respect.

The "whole woman" directs her power (ableness) in useful, productive, yet considerate ways.

Learning to communicate effectively involves utilizing the Princess Frog's masculine and feminine energy to serve her (and others) well. (Check out Assertiveness Training on the Web and see I-Statements in Appendix G: Confronting the Father)

Appendix G

CONFRONTING THE FATHER

Addressing the father in order to go on with her life in a healthier way is one of the greatest challenges for The Princess Frog; it takes courage. Why confront? To give voice to her wounding. To stand up for her Inner Child who was abandoned, betrayed, or rejected. There is great power in doing so; it is the path of the warrior. The experience will help The Princess Frog become more whole.

The Wise Woman needs to be the one who handles the father issue. Her wisdom and vision will carry the daughter through. She is the one who is capable of keeping the dreamy, naïve Maiden, the wounded, innocent Child, and even the harsh Judge out of it.

(See Appendix H: Acknowledging One's Parts)

How can the daughter prepare for this challenge? Certainly not by impulsively rushing in. She must begin by asking herself what she hopes to accomplish, and how she might proceed as a result. There are various possibilities. Generally, there are four issues to be addressed in confronting her father:

- The way in which she was wounded by him.
- Her feelings about it.
- How the event (or events) has impacted her life.
- What she wants from him now, if anything.

Some Suggestions:

The daughter will have the best chance of being heard by the father if she utilizes I-Statements. (To be explained shortly.)

No matter what her father may throw back at her, she can always say:

"I know you see it that way."

(This serves to let him know she's heard him, and it may possibly give him a clue that there is another way to see things.)

If her father mocks her for becoming tearful, she may respond:

"I see I have tears. This always happens when I'm dealing with something important." To claim, accept, value and stand up for one's tears is not a weakness. Tears are nature's way of saying something is getting touched in us. They are a gift if we recognize them as such.

It can be helpful to carry a touchstone (a lucky coin; a symbol of the daughter's adulthood and competency, such as a daybook; perhaps a piece of religious jewelry, etc.). Wearing a power color to give or signify her strength, painting her fingernails a bold color ... these can bring confidence. Wearing heels can give her a sense of height, making her feel "bigger," therefore more powerful. Even when confronting the father indirectly, as described below, these power tips can help The Princess Frog in her all-important task.

Addressing the father may be done directly or otherwise through the use of writing, fantasy, dreams, therapy, in relationship with other men, or by other creative means.

DIRECT CONFRONTATION

The Princess Frog may decide the time is right to express her feelings of abandonment, betrayal, etc. directly in the presence of her father. If she does, however, she needs to realize that her father's response may not be the one she has hoped for. It would be nice if he were accountable. It would be great if he listened and felt remorse. Unfortunately, it can be a disaster, and often is. There is **potential danger** in confronting her real father, in that he may respond to her in a re-wounding way: he may become defensive; he might not "get it"; he could turn on her and blame her; he may get physically or emotionally abusive.

Whatever he does, she needs to remind herself that she cannot control his behavior ... only hers. This isn't about him; it's about her standing up for herself. If she feels the direct route would prove too risky for any reason, finding another approach would make sense. This is not a failure on her part. She's protecting herself. That is called wisdom.

Upon reflection, depending on the nature of the abandonment she experienced and the kind of father she has, the daughter may decide to go ahead with her plan. She might bring someone along, perhaps to wait in the car, or be available afterwards for moral support. Performing the task, or attempting to do so with no expectations, keeps her focused on her task. Whether she gets the response she's longing for or not, her mission can be considered a triumph because she is facing her fear and standing up for her wounded Inner Child. In addition, any response her father provides, through word, behavior or lack thereof, can be considered important information for her in regard to his current character.

LETTER WRITING

As previously stated, sometimes, for safety reasons, it is ill-advised to confront the father directly. It also may not be possible. Perhaps the father has died or cannot be located. Or, he lives too far away, and practicality or economic considerations prohibit a visit. Maybe he has become senile or suffered a debilitating stroke. He could refuse to meet with his daughter.

When direct confrontation is not an option, depending on the situation, a letter (perhaps certified or registered), maybe even an email, might be a solution. This is less intimidating, and the daughter has the advantage of organizing her thoughts and staying on task without being interrupted or distracted. It can be preferable to first write a "no-holds-barred" sort of letter, in which The Princess Frog could let loose, without consideration for language, spelling or grammar. She may write in a frenzy, and spew out a barrage of swear words. This can actually be therapeutic. What would not be therapeutic, would be to mail it. For one thing, her father probably would not read past the first line. And secondly, she became wounded due to a lack of respect by her father; why stoop to that level now by not respecting herself enough to write in a decent manner?

After setting aside the first letter, she may need to write a few more until she is ready to write the one that will be sent. Unlike those not mailed, this letter will be written by her Wise Woman.

Even if the father is deceased or has become mentally incapacitated in some way, it can be a good exercise for the daughter to confront her father in a letter even though he will never read it or understand it. She is doing this for herself.

I-STATEMENTS (with Direct Confrontation or in Letter Writing)

Communication experts suggest using the "I-Statement" (owning one's feelings) as a tool to promote effective communication, rather than hinder it by using the "You-Statement" (blaming others). Essentially, the speaker's I-Statement is more likely to be listened to versus the speaker's You-Statement, which is more inclined to be interrupted with come backs, defensive in nature. The smartest thing The Princess Frog can do in this undertaking is remember to express her feelings instead of attacking her father. (This holds true in all communication.) No matter how the father responds ... whether with nasty comments, intimidation or blame ... if the daughter stays with I-Statements, she will have the greatest likelihood of being heard.

I have seen I-Statements presented in different ways. (I suggest you check out Assertiveness Training on the Web.) I have always used the following 3-part assertive I-Statement; it is neither passive nor aggressive:

Begin with: "I feel ...
followed by a feeling, such as: sad, scared, hurt, intimidated, confused, etc.

For example:
" I FEEL HURT ... "
> NOT: "I feel (one can substitute "think") you are an idiot."
> NOT: "I feel like (one can substitute "believe" or "think") you are an idiot."

"WHEN YOU ... "
followed by a behavior or action (what caused the feeling), such as:
> "I feel hurt WHEN YOU CALL ME NAMES."

"I WOULD LIKE IT IF YOU ... "
followed by a request. Other possibilities:
"I would appreciate it if you ... "
"It is important to me that you ... "
"I need you to ... "

Put together, it could look like this:
"I FEEL HURT WHEN YOU CALL ME NAMES. I WOULD LIKE YOU TO PLEASE STOP."

Or, you could reverse #s 1 and 2:
"WHEN YOU CALL ME NAMES, I FEEL HURT. I WOULD LIKE YOU TO PLEASE STOP."

When the Princess Frog confronts her father, she might say something like this, depending on what happened to her:

"I want to share something with you. When you left the family, I felt hurt and abandoned, and it has affected me deeply my entire life. I need you to be accountable for your part in what happened."

Remember, he might not give her what she desires in return, but she is presenting her case from a place of strength and truth. She can be proud of that, no matter the outcome. She can't control what he will do or say. She only can control how she conducts herself. In some cases, a simple statement like the one above, may be the gateway to a meaningful discussion, during which she continues to use I-Statements. In other cases, she may make her statement only to see it has not made the impact she had wished for. Should this happen, she may need to turn and walk away. Whatever the results of the confrontation, the daughter needs to praise herself for her courage.

Last word on I-Statements: they are comprised of masculine and feminine energy working in tandem. The masculine risks and confronts while the feminine considers the importance of making a connection. (See Appendix F: Using Masculine and Feminine Energy Effectively)

FANTASY

Addressing the father in fantasy might mean imagining a dialogue in which The Princess Frog confronts her father regarding her wounding. In this way, she gains a sense of power over, or resolution to, the situation.

As mentioned previously, the daughter could use her imagination in other ways as well. (See Appendix D: The Inner Child) She may picture herself as she is now, a grownup, and reflect back on the memory of what happened to her as a child. She can then "change" the incident by protecting the child she used to be. For example, she could imagine using her body as a shield by standing in front of the child. Or, she may have to get more physical. Clients I've had in the past have fantasized about restraining the father in different ways: tying him up, sitting on him, or striking him. One daughter put her father in a meat grinder.

Fantasy is one tool The Princess Frog may employ in her quest to heal. What makes this technique different from direct encounters and letter writing is that THESE FANTASIES SHOULD NEVER HAPPEN IN REALITY. This is a safe, often productive way to deal with one's feelings, where no one really gets hurt.

DREAMS

Facing the father in dreams is not about just having a dream in which he appears. It involves some sort of confrontation or resolution, through which the dreamer gains power. Often the father, or the incident he represents, is cloaked in the image of something other than himself. This is seen in the fairy tale, where snarling animals relentlessly chase the daughter. One of my clients experienced so many of these frightening dreams, before she was able to turn to face the oncoming wild dogs, and with her finger pointing at them, said these words in a strong voice: "What are you doing in my dream?" She never had the dream again. When she stood up to her fears, she conquered them. (See Appendix B: Dreams)

THERAPY

Therapy provides the safe arena in which to do the work. The therapist acts as coach, guide, and witness. And often as a lifeline. She or he is there to help the daughter come out of the forest of her confusion, hopelessness, and despair in a more whole way.

RELATIONSHIPS WITH OTHER MEN

Confronting men who abuse her, relinquishing relationships that don't feel good, looking for men who honor and respect her ... these are ways in which The Princess Frog can make a stand for herself.

Before the shift occurred, the father may have been somewhat nurturing, caring, attentive, available, and boundaried. Because he changed, does not mean that good part of him initially experienced by the daughter need be totally lost. She can decide to reclaim it by treating herself and others with love and respect. She can also fantasize The Good Father comforting her when her Inner Child is in pain … just as it might have happened before she was abandoned and set adrift.

OTHER CREATIVE MEANS

Painting, dancing, story boarding, poetry and song writing … these have all been used by daughters in the search to heal their wounding.

Appendix H

ACKNOWLEDGING ONE'S PARTS

A Princess Frog out of touch with the various aspects of herself will potentially have an internal conflict. Her unidentified or unrespected parts can sabotage and adversely affect both herself and others in the process. What is ignored will cause trouble by way of anxiety or difficulties in interpersonal relationships. Once the daughter is aware of and honors what "lives" within, she has the opportunity for integration, which leads to balance and wholeness.

In the fairy tale, there is a discussion among the parts of The Princess Frog, as to who will be in charge of steering the boat. Each has his or her point of view. As explained, these components represent pieces of ourselves, which drive us.

When dealing with an important issue, the daughter may use this method in her decision-making. For example, if the daughter goes to a party, she can have a good time, yet keep her wits about her:

The Wise Woman is the part of The Princess Frog connected to good self-care, wholeness, and consciousness. She sees the big picture, making sure the daughter comes to, spends time at, and returns home from the party safely. She limits The Princess Frog's drinking. She makes sure the daughter always brings along I.D. and money in case of an emergency.

In charge, The Wise Woman may allow **The Maiden** to attend the party, but limits her participation, due to her naiveté. Some flirting may be okay; going to bed with someone she barely knows, is not. Many a woman has become unhappily pregnant or cast aside, after having been swept off her feet. As compared with men, women are more likely to bond with sex. This is no doubt connected to their need to be able to bond with their babies. For this reason, it is particularly important for a woman to think carefully before jumping into bed with a man prior to knowing what kind of person he is. The Princess Frog has been wounded; therefore she has a blind spot when it comes to men. She must protect herself so she doesn't get re-wounded.

The Wise Woman would not invite **The Judge** to the party … devaluing The Princess Frog is not allowed! **The Inner Child,** unless the party is somewhere like Disneyland, would not be included, though **The Man** might be along to watch the clock and help solve any problems that may arise.

The following is another example of how to work with one's parts; when going for a job interview, imagine the following:

The Wise Woman would be in charge. **The Man** could make sure of a prompt arrival. **The Inner Child** and **The Maiden** would be sent to spend time with a responsible, loving friend, where The Child could play and The Maiden could watch a romantic movie on T.V. **The Judge** would be sent to the moon, trapped in a box, etc.

The more real the daughter makes these parts, the better the result. For example, if she is scared, she can calm herself down by picturing her Inner Child on her lap, etc. These reminders can keep the daughter from getting into situations that would cause her fear in the first place. That's because she is beginning to think ahead. In time, the necessity of using one's parts diminishes, as healthy habits become second nature and The Princess Frog becomes more whole.

The Detective

There is another component of The Princess Frog that is not discussed in the fairy tale. It is a part closely aligned with The Wise Woman, called "The Detective."

A real-life detective is a person who not only gathers facts, but, in order to do the job well, holds these facts to be of great importance. Taking notes, documenting findings, etc. keep the detective in his or her head. It is a thinking exercise, not an emotional one.

The Princess Frog can utilize this piece of herself to keep from slipping into a feeling state. The Detective operates in the adult part of the daughter largely as an observer or analyst. It can keep her from "going under the spell" of the emotional Child or the scattered Maiden. Finding interest in all that surrounds her usually works. She may even start asking probing questions in her mind, as to what she is observing. The more CURIOUS she becomes and the more FASCINATED she is by everything she sees occurring, the more likely she will keep her cool and stay in her head. This is a handy way to avoid falling into a trance state (See Appendix E: Trance States), and is a useful trick when dealing with seductive men. Being in the role of The Detective can also serve her well when facing the father. (See Appendix G: Confronting The Father)

Appendix I

SYMBOLS OF WOUNDING AND HEALING

Through the years as a practicing licensed psychotherapist, I've asked women to draw symbols of what their initial wounding looked like, and at a later point, what their healing looked like.

The following pages reveal the work of eight such women. Their names are changed to protect their identities:

P: Polly
R: Renee
I: Iris
N: Nancy
C: Cynthia
E: Elaine
S: Sandy
S: Sharon

These women experienced a dramatic shift when their fathers altered the healthy boundary that needed to exist between them and their daughters.

For the first drawing, the client was asked to close her eyes and allow a symbol to come to her, which represented the shift in the relationship with her father. Then she was asked to draw or sketch this symbol.

For the second drawing, the client was asked to close her eyes and allow a symbol to come to her, which represented the healing she had experienced in relation to her father or men. If she hadn't yet experienced healing, what would these relationships look like if they were healed? The client was then asked to draw or sketch that symbol.

"POLLY" named her parents' divorce as the cause of her wounding in her relationship with her father. She describes her dad as "warm and loving" before the shift, which occurred when she was six. She was traumatized by his absences as her parents struggled whether to stay together or not. The shift came "probably when he left home and my mother and I moved in with my grandmother." After the shift, he was affectionate, but unpredictable as to when that would occur.

The symbol that came to Polly's mind was a pair of white shoes:

> These are little girls' white shoes. I have a strong memory of my father not wanting to pick me up when I had these shoes on, or putting me down quickly for fear that the white of the shoes would somehow 'dirty' the blue suit he was wearing.

It is interesting to note that the divorce was the shift, but the shoes are the symbol of it.

In a later healing drawing, Polly depicts herself sitting on a bench with her father. He is not looking at her, though she may be looking at him. They are not sitting close together, however he has his arm stretched out, with his hand around her shoulder and they are both smiling. He is saying, "I love you very much. I did the very best I could." Of her drawing, Polly expresses that "maybe a slight bit of healing [has] occurred." She states that the white shoes being off her feet could represent "a step toward wellness."

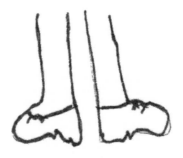

"Polly"

"Polly"

"RENEE" cannot remember exactly when the shift occurred, but before it did, her life looked like this:

> My father worked most of the time but when I did see him, he was neutral to me. He did drink much of the time, and I remember he and my mother arguing quite a bit.

When Renee was twelve years old, she and her father began to spend more time together. It was at this point she noticed the shift:

> He and I would go to the beach. When I became a 'young lady,' a sexual being, my father recognized me more. I knew he was attracted to attractive women and I guess I wanted to be attractive to him and other men. That was how I would be accepted and be a part of a busy man's life.

Renee drew an erotic symbol: a feminine image with its flowing, watery, curvaceous lines.

In her healing drawing, Renee drew a circular shape. Within it are two hands. She notes, it is "an incomplete circle, yet a sense of both parties reaching out in an effort of getting closer." Though there is space between the hands, black lines join them. Her father's hand on the left is drawn darker and appears to be reaching out more than her right hand. The sense of preserving a boundary on her part is clear.

Renee made these final comments as she completed her therapy:

> I feel that I have had good relationships with men but that I have in the past had to make sacrifices for the sake of the man. I don't do that anymore. I have become more assertive and have found that I as well as the man in my life can deal with being comfortable/uncomfortable together.

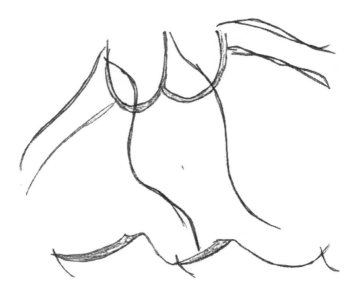

"Renee"

"Renee"

"IRIS" also experienced a divorce as a "sub-shift" as compared to the death of her father. Her father died when she was quite young. Until that time, she had pleasant memories and an overall positive relationship with him:

> I adored him and he adored me. He focused on me, and I felt protected and surrounded by love. When I was two and a half, my parents divorced, but I never felt a change in his attention or caring, though I missed him badly. The more major shift was when he died when I was seven and a half. I was devastated and lonely, suffering a lot. I lost a very important aspect of having attention paid to me. So I felt smaller ... A great and gaping emptiness was hovering above me, gray and empty.

Iris drew a symbol of departure, wherein her father is shrinking farther and farther away from her "in Heaven." She says, "Daddy, don't leave me!" He responds, "I'm sorry. I have to go." Both are crying, their mouths turned down, their hearts broken. It is a pencil drawing except for yellow-crayon beams of light emanating from a line that curves just in front of his outstretched arms. Her arms likewise reach for him.

Iris comments that she and her father reach for each other and are never able to connect again, as he fades away ... "while I have to stay here on the ground."

Her healing picture shows her and her father reaching out for each other. The dialogue between them is one of equality and acknowledgement of their healthy separateness, as evidenced by their different colors: she is drawn in magenta, he in green. Like Polly's picture, this is a common depiction in which there is a meeting of sorts between father and daughter.

At the end of therapy, Iris commented:

> A big shift has occurred in the past months. I gained a lot of understanding about how I had been viewing men. I've always chosen men who are unattainable. I can see now how the unhealthy part of me acts out (rather, wants to act out) in a stimulating circumstance. The difference is now I can catch it inside and not actually do anything. I can really say no to it. That is progress.

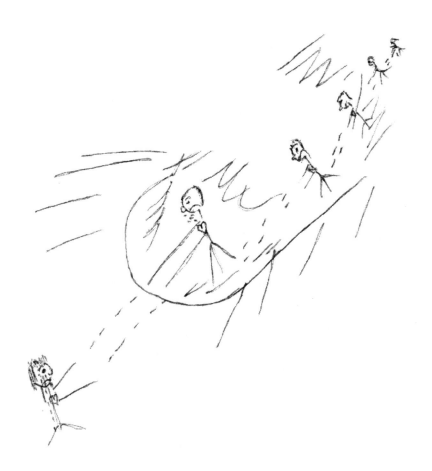

"Iris"

"Iris"

"NANCY," at age fourteen, also became dethroned as princess when her father died. Before his death, her dad was hospitalized on and off for two years. After he died, she says, "my life turned upside down. I suddenly was left completely on my own."

The symbol Nancy used to reflect the shift tells her story in three parts. In her early years to the left, she's smiling in front of her house. The sun is shining and smoke is coming out of the chimney, lending a sense of warmth. The path leading to the house bears the name "Childhood." In the middle of the page, an arrow points to an abstract, somewhat explosive configuration, labeled "Death" and "Chaos." The right side of the page shows Nancy in four stages of development, from shortest to tallest, each with unhappy expressions above the words: "Grow up fast and alone."

For her healing symbol, Nancy made a pencil drawing of an interaction between two characters in the classic story: *The Little Prince* by Antoine de Saint Exupery. The relationship between the prince and the fox that meet, and then part, is her model for healing her relationship with her deceased father. She has begun to let go of her Ideal Father and move forward as herself instead of as a woman who identifies herself so strongly with her father.

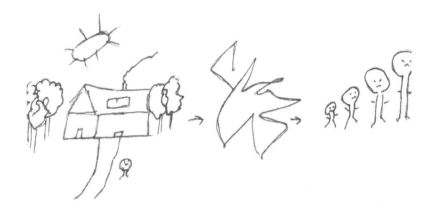

"Nancy"

"Nancy"

"CYNTHIA" was a kind of princess in that she believed she was special, as evidenced by her father's pleasure in seeing her and by his spending time with her. She saw him as a role model ... "great" and "wonderful." When she was twelve years old, she experienced a shift in the relationship:

> My father called to me as I passed his room. I was eager to go to him and hoped we would play again, but he began feeling my breasts and making sexual comments. My breasts were appreciated on his part and his comments were shocking to me.

After the shift, things were different:

> I tried to stay away from him. I didn't know what to do when he was there and I was lost when he was away. I hated myself for being confused and unable to make the relationship 'work.' I couldn't ask for anything from him because I hated him, too.

The symbol Cynthia drew to represent the shift is of a dripping heart. There is a strong sense of wounding, ripping, and collapse. It also appears as if fumes are rising above it, like one sees after an explosion or cave-in. The drawing is done with a black ballpoint pen.

A couple of years previously, Cynthia had drawn a different picture of the shift. She drew her lifeline from birth to the present and into the projected future. At her twelve-year-old mark, she placed a giant crack that continued across the bottom half of the paper, reaching and splintering progressively outward like a black, spindly spider.

Fragmenting images of the shift reveal the devastation on the psyche by abandoning fathers who inappropriately turn toward their daughters.

For her healing drawing, Cynthia drew a circular image with a pale lavender center that bursts into bright yellow beams, some of which have star-like tips. Black lines surround it, giving it a firecracker-in-the-night quality: "light breaking through the darkness." Circular images can represent wholeness.

"Cynthia"

"Cynthia"

"ELAINE" had adored her father:

> I was extremely close to him. I looked
> up to him for the love, safety, and
> affection that were not coming from
> my mother. I idolized him.

The shift occurred when Elaine was twelve and a half years old:

> It was his nervous breakdown from
> alcohol and drugs, and his emotional
> withdrawal from alcoholism.

After the shift, she wanted to "take care of him, help him, and be his parent."

Elaine drew a couple of symbols. She depicted a flower turning into a weed, and a boulder becoming sand. Next to the images she wrote:

> The magical thinking of innocence and
> belief turns into falling from a building
> that is precipitously placed.

Her sobering images allude to crumbling and decay.

Elaine shows healing symbols in a later drawing: "a house-church in relation to the father, and a balanced seesaw vis-à-vis men in general." She speaks of working on her father issues as "a process," and reports she now has "a foundation of spirituality," which serves to ground her.

"Elaine"

"Elaine"

"SANDY," another daughter of an alcoholic, describes her father before the shift occurred:

> He was the one presenting a sense of hope for me. I loved him and liked to be physically close to him. He responded, though possibly feeling discomfort about his sexual feelings toward me. I ended up feeling bad after having felt really good about his physical closeness (sitting on his lap, etc.)

She believes the shift came when she was in school, around the age of six or seven. Then, around age twelve, she "realized emotionally that he was not reliable, and I was left feeling betrayed." She says she "continued to be a wife-daughter in many ways until his death."

Sandy's symbol shows her (drawn in brown) sitting on the floor unhappily watching her father (drawn in blue) who has his back to her. She writes: "I'm sitting sadly, as my father walks away."

This father, struggling with his sexual feelings, set up a confusing sort of barrier, leaving her feel betrayed, "bad" and emotionally cut off.

For her healing drawing, Sandy drew a radiant mandala-like image of silver, red, pink, blue, orange, peach and lime. Mandalas can represent wholeness and spiritual transformation.

At the close of therapy, Sandy made this statement:

> I am now shifting through my feelings toward men and feel that I am aware of my issues of abandonment and betrayal. I am now starting to exercise my choices when I get frightened about the above.

"Sandy"

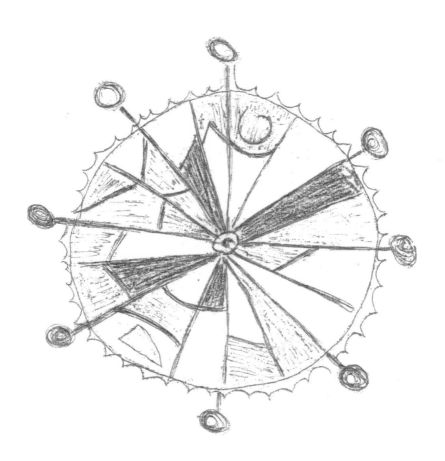

"Sandy"

"SHARON" felt a double shift, as did Iris and Sandy. She first experienced her parents' marital strife at ages seven to twelve; then the death of her father when she was fifteen. When she was very young, she had spent a lot of time with her dad, playing with him, learning new things, talking together.

When the arguing started between her parents, Sharon shifted to becoming afraid of her father at times and tried to stay away from him when he was angry with her mother.

When he died:

> I had no one to ask questions about
> him, questions only he could answer.
> Also, I needed support, being a teen
> and he wasn't there. I wanted Mom and
> Dad to be there, and he wasn't.

The symbol for her relationship with her father was a guitar. At first "the rhythm was pretty and in tune." Then it became "awful to hear—scary music." Finally, "the music stopped; he passed on to heaven."

In this case, the father was never personally inappropriate to his daughter. On the contrary, he was always directly involved with Sharon in a caring way. But the problem he had with his wife affected his daughter. In that respect, he failed as a protector.

In her healing drawing, Sharon once again draws a guitar as a symbol of her father. "Now the song is a continuous, flowing, happy one—not a song that keeps changing chords or songs."

As for men, she shows herself as a pail with a lid on top. She used to receive men's "garbage." Now she can recognize garbage when she sees it. The lid acts as a boundary. Her relationships are better as a result.

"Sharon"

"Sharon"